MENTAL MATHS HOMEWORK
FOR 11 YEAR OLDS

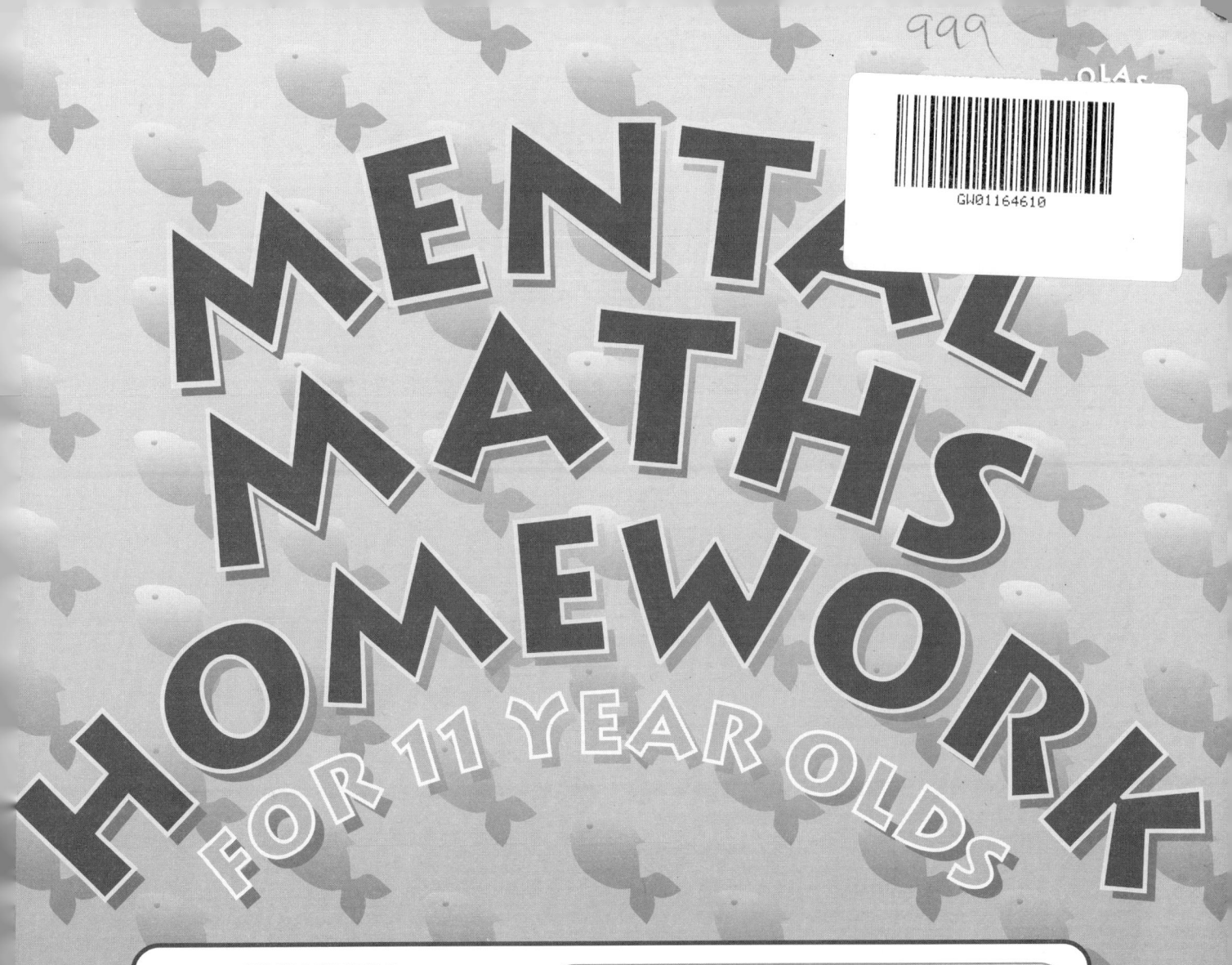

SERIES EDITOR
Lin Taylor
The IMPACT Project, University of North London Enterprises Ltd

AUTHOR
Kate Frood

EDITOR
Joel Lane

ASSISTANT EDITOR
Clare Miller

SERIES DESIGNER
Anna Oliwa

DESIGNER
Rachael Hammond

ILLUSTRATIONS
Mike Miller

COVER ARTWORK
James Alexander/David Oliver
Berkeley Studios

Text © 1999 Kate Frood
© 1999 Scholastic Ltd

Designed using Adobe Pagemaker
Published by Scholastic Ltd, Villiers House, Clarendon Avenue, Leamington Spa, Warwickshire CV32 5PR

1 2 3 4 5 6 7 8 9 0   9 0 1 2 3 4 5 6 7 8

British Library Cataloguing-in-Publication Data
A catalogue record for this book is available from the British Library.

ISBN 0-439-01707-6

The right of Kate Frood to be identified as the author of this work has been asserted by her in accordance with the Copyright, Designs and Patents Act 1988.

All rights reserved. This book is sold subject to the condition that it shall no, by way of trade or otherwise, be lent, hired out or otherwise circulated without the publisher's prior consent in any form of binding or cover other than that in which it is published and without a similar condition, including this condition, being imposed upon the subsequent purchaser.

No part of this publication may be reproduced, stored in a retrieval system, or transmitted, in any form or by any means, electronic, mechanical, photocopying, recording or otherwise, without the prior permission of the publisher. This book remains copyright, although permission is granted to copy pages 9–48 for classroom distribution and use only in the school which has purchased the book and in accordance with the CLA licensing agreement. Photocopying permission is given only for purchasers and not for borrowers of books from any lending service.

CONTENTS

INTRODUCTION 3
TEACHERS' NOTES 5

COUNTING AND ORDERING

SQUARE DANCE	9	knowing square numbers and square roots
MILLIONAIRE	10	understanding place value
LENGTH CHART	11	working with metric units of length
PRIME TARGET 1	12	identifying prime numbers
PRIME TARGET 2	13	extending knowledge of prime numbers
THE POINT IS 5	14	multiplying and dividing by 10, 100 or 1000
THE POINT IS 5 GAMEBOARD	15	
DOES IT GO?	16	identifying multiples
DOES IT GO? GAMEBOARD	17	
SUBTRACTAFACTA	18	identifying factors
FRACTION CHANCE	19	spotting relationships between fractions
DICEY DIVIDE	20	expressing fractions as decimals
DICEY DIVIDE: BINGO CARDS	21	
BREAKFAST CHALLENGE	22	understanding percentages
HAPPY NUMBERS	23	learning squares of numbers

ADDITION AND SUBTRACTION

WHO DARES WINS	24	practising quick mental addition
GOAL!	25	using estimation and mental addition
PYRAMID PROBLEM 1	26	using mental addition to solve a problem
PYRAMID PROBLEM 2	27	using mental subtraction to solve a problem

MULTIPLICATION AND DIVISION

TABLES PATIENCE	28	using rapid recall of multiplication facts
PYRAMID PATIENCE	29	using rapid recall of multiplication facts
THE WELSH BORDERS RACE	30	using multiplication to solve a problem
ESTIMATE	31	multiplying 2-digit numbers
MISSION IMPOSSIBLE?	32	using multiplication to solve a problem
GRIDLOCK!	33	using multiplication and division logically
MILLIONS	34	estimating results of multiplying large numbers
THE ANSWER TO EVERYTHING	35	using multiplication facts
FACTORS AND MULTIPLES	36	identifying factors and multiples
GRAB	37	recalling or working out multiples

MULTISTEP AND MIXED OPERATIONS

1999	38	using all four number operations
1, 3, 5, 7, 9	39	using all four number operations
FAIR SHARES	40	choosing and using number operations
CALENDAR MAGIC	41	using all four number operations
MATHS TENNIS	42	recalling number facts for all operations
'STAY THE SAME' NUMBERS	43	reasoning about number operations
MYSTERY SQUARE	44	using number relationships logically
SNAP!	45	working with unknown numbers
HAPPY BIRTHDAY!	46	using a range of mental skills
SIX STEPS TO 1000	47	using number operations strategically

LETTER TO HELPER 48

ABOUT HOMEWORK

Homework can be a very useful opportunity to practise and develop children's understanding of the work done in school. Games and maths challenges can be very good activities to share with someone at home, especially to develop mental maths strategies and maths language skills. Research* indicates that parental involvement is a major factor in children's educational success. Most parents want to help their children with their school work, but often do not know how and 'traditional' homework does not involve parents. Shared homework activities, such as can be found in *Mental Maths Homework*, are designed to be completed with a parent or helper, such as a sibling, neighbour or other adult who can work with the child. Working one-to-one with an adult in the home environment really has a powerful effect. The National Numeracy Strategy strongly supports this type of homework, which is in line with a variety of government guidelines on the role of parents and making home links.

ABOUT MENTAL MATHS AT HOME

Mental Maths Homework is particularly concerned to develop children's *mental* mathematics. In order to become competent at mental calculation, children need to talk about mathematics and try out different strategies, as well as to practise number facts and skills. Children explaining their mathematics to a parent or helper can help to clarify and develop their understanding of the mathematics. This type of homework, developed by The IMPACT Project, is a *joint* activity: the helper and child working together.

ABOUT MENTAL MATHS HOMEWORK

This series comprises of six books, one for each age group from 6–11 years (Year 1/P2–Year 6/P7). Each book contains 36 photocopiable activities – enough for one to be sent home each week throughout the school year, if you wish. The activities concentrate on the number system and developing children's calculation strategies and are designed to fit into your planning, whatever scheme you are using. Since these books are designed to support the same aims of developing mental maths strategies and vocabulary, they make an ideal follow-on to the class work outlined in Scholastic's other *Mental Maths* series. The objectives for each activity are based on those in the National Numeracy Strategy *Framework for Teaching Mathematics* and the content is appropriate for teachers following other UK curriculum documents.

USING THE ACTIVITIES IN SCHOOL

Although the books are designed for a particular age group they should be used flexibly so that the right level of activity is set for a child or class. All the activities are photocopiable: most are one page, some are two, or require an extra resource page (to be found at the back of the book) for certain games or number card activities. The activities for older children will generally take longer than those for younger children.

BEFORE

It is essential that each activity is introduced to the class before it is sent home with them. This fulfils several crucial functions. It enables the child to explain the activity to the parent or carer; ensuring the child understands the task. It also familiarizes the child with the activity; developing motivation and making the activity more accessible. This initial introduction to the activity can be done as part of a regular maths lesson, at the end of the day, or whenever fits in with your class's routine.

AFTER

It is also important that the child brings something back to school from the activity at home. This will not necessarily be substantial, or even anything written, since the activities aim to develop mental mathematics. It is equally important that what the child brings in from home is genuinely valued by you. It is unlikely that parents will be encouraged to share activities with their children if they do not feel that their role is valued either. Each activity indicates what should be brought back to school, and the teachers' notes (on pages 5–8) offer guidance on introducing and working with or reviewing the outcome of each activity.

HELPERS

All the activities have a note to the helper explaining the purpose of the activity and how to help the child, often emphasizing useful vocabulary. The helpers' notes also give indications of how to adapt the activity at home, and what to do if the child gets stuck. Many of the activities are games or fun activities which it is hoped that the parent and child will enjoy doing together and will do again, even when not set for homework, thus increasing the educational benefit. It is particularly beneficial for a game to be played a number of times.

OTHER WAYS TO USE THE ACTIVITIES

The activities offered in *Mental Maths Homework* are very flexible and will be used in different ways in different schools. As well as being used for shared homework, they could form the basis of a display or a school challenge, or be used as activities for a maths club. Or, they could be used independently of the school situation by parents who wish to provide stimulating and appropriate educational activities for their children.

USING THE ACTIVITIES AT HOME

If you are a parent using these activities outside of school:

- Choose an activity you both think looks interesting and get going straight away with your child. Make the work *joint*: the helper and the child working out what has to be done *together*.
- Read the instructions to your child and ask him or her to explain what has to be done. It is very effective for the child to do the explaining.

USING HOMEWORK DIARIES

Developing a dialogue between teacher and parent is an important part of shared homework. By working with the child at home, the parent becomes more familiar with the mathematics of the classroom. The teacher also needs to hear from the parent about how the child is faring with the activities. Diaries provide a very good mechanism for this. The helpers and/or the children can comment on the activities (which will give you important feedback) and individual targets can be put into the diary. The diaries can act, therefore, as an important channel of communication. (See below for details about finding out more information about diaries.)

ABOUT THIS BOOK

In *Mental Maths Homework for 11 year olds*, all the activities practise and extend essential numeracy skills described in the Year 6 key objectives of the National Numeracy Strategy *Framework for Teaching Mathematics*. This book includes, for example, activities on working with decimals, using percentages and proportion and increasing the children's capability with the four operations. The aims include developing checking strategies (such as estimating the answers to long multiplication and division calculations before carrying them out) and being able to follow and perform longer sequences of instructions to solve problems. The 'key objectives' are challenging: the level set is that children are attaining the NC Level 4 expectations and are beginning to work within Level 5. These levels are equivalent to Levels D and E in the Scottish National Guidelines for *Mathematics 5–14*. For some Year 6/Primary 7 pupils, it may be more appropriate to use *Mental Maths Homework* activities ...*for 9 year olds* or ...*for 10 year olds*.

It is assumed that the children have a good grasp of all the key mental maths skills described in the *Framework* for Year 5, and are now (in Year 6/Primary 7) working to extend and consolidate these skills. It is assumed, for example, that the children know the multiplication facts to 10 × 10, can relate fractions to decimals and can round decimals (to one or two decimal places) to the nearest integer, as well as being increasingly confident with the four operations.

Children involved in the National Numeracy Strategy will be receiving regular mental maths practice in the first part of the daily mathematics lesson. These homework activities provide a range of contexts for extra practice and consolidation, with particular emphasis on developing the relevant language.

---

* Bastiani, J. & Wolfendale, S. (1996) *Home-School Work: Review, Reflection and Development* David Fulton Publishers.

THE IMPACT PROJECT

The activities in *Mental Maths Homework* have all been devised by members of The IMPACT Project, based at the University of North London. The project, a pioneer of shared homework, with a wealth of experience, is involved in a variety of initiatives concerning parental involvement and homework. It also supports schools in setting up a school framework for shared homework. If you would like help with developing shared homework, planning a whole-school framework for homework or developing mental mathematics at home and at school, maybe through INSET with experienced providers, contact The IMPACT Project. Information about other activities undertaken by the project and about other IMPACT books and resources, such as the IMPACT diaries, is also available from The IMPACT Project.

The IMPACT Project
University of North London
School of Education
166–220 Holloway Road
London
N7 8DB

tel. no. 0171 753 7052

fax. no. 0171 753 5420

e-mail: impact-enquiries@unl.ac.uk
impact-orders@unl.ac.uk

web: http://www.unl.ac.uk/impact

COUNTING & ORDERING

SQUARE DANCE
OBJECTIVE: To recognize squares and square roots of numbers.
BEFORE: Revise the sequence of square numbers. Then draw the 0–9 grid on an OHT or board and play a game against the class, choosing individual children to cross out numbers. Encourage the children to think about how they might beat their helpers.
AFTER: Ask the children to report back on who won at home. Replay the game in class to see whether any winning strategies have been found.

MILLIONAIRE
OBJECTIVE: To know what each digit in a six-digit number represents. To develop calculator skills.
BEFORE: The children should have worked on numbers to 1,000,000 and been asked to identify the value of a specified digit. Play a game against the class, ideally using an OHP calculator to demonstrate; the children can play against you in pairs. Go round the class, asking how much each pair owes you.
AFTER: Ask the children to tell you who won at home. Replay the game in pairs.

LENGTH CHART
OBJECTIVE: To multiply and divide whole numbers and decimals by 10, 100 and 1000. To choose suitable units to estimate or measure length.
BEFORE: Make sure the children understand how the place value system works, and how different metric measures are related. Practise moving digits up and down the place value chart: ×100, ÷10 and so on. Ask the class to estimate some lengths and distances, and to suggest appropriate units. Ask for estimates of the longest ever fingernail, then reveal the truth!
AFTER: A large class chart could be drawn up to share the children's work.

PRIME TARGET 1
OBJECTIVE: To recognize prime numbers. To investigate a general statement.
BEFORE: The children need to know what prime numbers are and be able to identify those under 100 (using tests of divisibility). With the class, model a systematic way to approach the problem. Highlight that the statement doesn't work for 1. Suggest that it looks false, and challenge the children to find other numbers it doesn't work for (27 and 35 are the next two).
AFTER: Share the results on a class chart.

PRIME TARGET 2
OBJECTIVE: To recognize prime numbers. To solve a mathematical puzzle.
BEFORE: This follows on from 'Prime target 1'. Ask the class to recall all the prime numbers under 100 (orally). List them on the board. Write some higher numbers and ask for reasonable guesses as to whether they are prime.
AFTER: Create a display of all possible answers. The lowest answer I know of is 225 (from 5 + 47 + 29 + 61 + 83). Can your class beat me?

THE POINT IS 5
OBJECTIVE: To multiply and divide whole numbers and decimals by 10, 100 and 1000.
BEFORE: This game follows on from 'Millionaire' and 'Length chart'. The children will need to be confident in multiplying and dividing decimals by multiples of 10. Play with the whole class, using an OHP, a grid drawn on the board or a large piece of paper. Move around the board, asking members of the class to say what each number has to be divided by to make the move. Reinforce their knowlege of place value.
AFTER: Use an enlarged version of the gameboard as a starter for quick mental and oral work. Point to numbers and ask the children to tell you which operation is needed.

DOES IT GO?
OBJECTIVE: To recognize multiples. To know and apply tests of divisibility.
BEFORE: The children will need to know how to recognize multiples of 2, 3, 4, 5, 6, 8, 9 and 10. Revise these tests of divisibility. Display a game board on an OHT, paper or a chalkboard. Beside each number, note its factors. Play a game against the whole class. Which numbers are easy? Which are hard? Use the words **factor** and **multiple** as often as you can.
AFTER: Test the children's knowledge of factors as a mental and oral starter to a maths lesson using 0–9 digit cards.

SUBTRACTAFACTA
OBJECTIVE: To identify factors and multiples. To think strategically.
BEFORE: Revise factors with quick-fire mental questions. Play the game against the whole class to make sure that they are clear about the rules. Use the words **factor** and **multiple** as often as you can.
AFTER: Discuss any winning strategies the children have found. Play again against members of the class as a plenary activity.

FRACTION CHANCE
OBJECTIVE: To recognize relationships between fractions.
BEFORE: Introduce this game by playing it against the whole class, with one child rolling for them. Go through what possible fractions could be scored. Revise addition of fractions.
AFTER: Use the children's score sheets to explore the different ways they made 1.

DICEY DIVIDE
OBJECTIVE: To use decimal notation, knowing what each digit represents. To express a quotient as a decimal fraction.
BEFORE: The children should be familiar with the decimal quotients for $\frac{5}{6}$, $\frac{3}{4}$ and so on. With the class, find all the possible pairs of numbers you might roll with two dice. List these on the board and then, together, calculate the quotients as decimals. Encourage estimates, and model how to use paper and pencil division methods.
AFTER: Create a fractions domino game using decimal and fractional equivalents.

BREAKFAST CHALLENGE
OBJECTIVE: To understand percentages. To solve a problem involving proportion.
BEFORE: Do a quick survey in class to find out the variety of cereals eaten at home. Discuss terms such as **vitamins** and **RDA**. Explain the task and work through an example altogether. Model how to do an easy calculation (100% ÷ 50%) and a hard one (100% ÷ 17%).
AFTER: When the data has been returned, there are opportunities for data handling work and links with health education. Go on to look at the salt and sugar content of cereal.

HAPPY NUMBERS
OBJECTIVE: To know squares of numbers. To use knowledge of number facts to add numbers mentally.
BEFORE: This homework follows on from 'Square dance'. The children will need to know the squares of the numbers 1–9 by heart. Model the activity with the whole class, using an OHP or board: ask the children to suggest start numbers and work through the number chain, doing the mental calculations together. Show the class how chains can interlink, and how to organize their investigation and findings.
AFTER: Compile the children's results on a whole-class chart or diagram.

ADDITION & SUBTRACTION

WHO DARES WINS
OBJECTIVE: To use knowledge of number facts to add numbers mentally.
BEFORE: Play a game against the whole class. Make sure that the children check whether the lower two-digit number will land them on a multiple of 100, rather than going for the higher number every time.
AFTER: Test the children's knowledge of the number bonds of multiples of 100 as a mental and oral starter to the lesson. For example: 72 + ? = 100 and 243 + ? = 300.

GOAL!
OBJECTIVE: To solve a problem using estimation and strategies for mental addition and subtraction.
BEFORE: Model appropriate strategies by working through a similar problem. *Together: Amit and Ben are aged 31; Ben and Chloe are aged 26; Chloe and Danielle are aged 17; Danielle and Eddie are aged 27; Amit, Chloe and Eddie are aged 42.* Solution: A = 14, B = 17, C = 9, D = 8, E = 19.
Discuss **reasonable guesses** and explain how the last sum is the key.
AFTER: Discuss the solutions found to the homework problem. The correct solution is: A = 47, B = 53, C = 29, D = 56, E = 34.

PYRAMID PROBLEM 1
OBJECTIVE: To solve a problem using mental strategies for addition.
BEFORE: Activities of this kind are an excellent warm-up for a maths lesson. Draw a pyramid on the board with five numbers in the base and ask the class either to add up neighbouring numbers until a top number is reached or (as in the homework) to find the difference between neighbouring numbers. The level of difficulty can be changed by altering the base numbers. The homework will extend this basic activity.
AFTER: Share the children's answers. A top score of 16 can be made with the base numbers (L–R): 93, 68, 74, 21, 50.

PYRAMID PROBLEM 2
OBJECTIVE: To solve a problem using mental strategies for subtraction.
BEFORE: This activity follows on from 'Pyramid problem 1'. Make sure the children understand how the rules of the two challenges differ. Have a go as a class beforehand, making sure you get it wrong!
AFTER: Share the children's answers. The highest top score I reached was 66, from the base numbers (L–R): 76, 54, 32, 10, 98.

MULTIPLICATION & DIVISION

TABLES PATIENCE
OBJECTIVE: To use rapid recall of multiplication facts. To recognize factors.
BEFORE: Gather the children around you and play a demonstration game, asking them to help you identify factors. Can they explain why 36 and 60 are good target numbers while 37 and 61 are not?
AFTER: Use this as a mental or oral starter to a lesson. Write 36 and 60 on the board. Divide the class into a 36 team and a 60 team. How many different ways can each team find to make their number using multiplication only?

PYRAMID PATIENCE
OBJECTIVE: To use rapid recall of multiplication facts.
BEFORE: Model a game with the whole class, asking them to predict what cards you need. Explain that the 10 card represents zero. Encourage the children to keep trying – it is hard to 'beat the pack' and finish!
AFTER: This activity links well with class work on last-digit number patterns.

THE WELSH BORDERS RACE
OBJECTIVE: To use multiplication facts. To approach a number problem logically.
BEFORE: The class will need clear guidance on how to approach this problem systematically. For example:

Guess for 3rd fence	heads	legs
19 horses	19	76
7 riders	7	14
	26	90 ➡ too many legs

Help the children to see that 36 heads at the start means 18 horses and 18 riders. This gives them a basis for later estimates.
AFTER: Share answers and strategies. The solution is: After the third fence, 15 horses and 11 riders continued, so 11 horses still had riders. At the finishing line, there were 7 horses and 5 riders, so 2 horses were unmounted.

ESTIMATE
OBJECTIVE: To use knowledge of number facts and place value to multiply 2-digit numbers both mentally (estimating answers) and on paper.
BEFORE: This is the hardest multiplication activity in this book. Play a few rounds with the whole class in which every member of the class makes an estimate. Ask individuals to explain their estimates. Model how to do long multiplication.
AFTER: Discuss estimation strategies. Model some long multiplication, asking for estimates first; encourage the use of effective strategies for reaching estimates.

MISSION IMPOSSIBLE?
OBJECTIVE: To multiply numbers both mentally (estimating answers) and on paper. To approach a number problem logically.
BEFORE: Model how to tackle the problem systematically (as shown in the 'Dear Helper' note). Ask questions to get the children thinking, such as: *Would six Dollies be a good guess?*
AFTER: The answer is 1 Dribble Dolly, 49 Yorky Yoyos and 50 Slime Worms. The 'Bet you can't' challenge could be undertaken as a follow-up in class.

GRIDLOCK!
OBJECTIVE: To know multiplication and division facts by heart. To use these to solve number problems.
BEFORE: The key to this problem is seeing where to start: the row of six ticks equals 30, so one tick must be 30 ÷ 6 = 5. Now look at the column of ticks and flowers: one flower must be 1. It is best to lead the children this far in a whole-class introduction, so that they feel they have made a start.
AFTER: Go through the children's results later in the week. The answers are: flower = 1, triangle = 2, cross = 3, raindrop = 4, tick = 5, square = 6, arrow = 7, face = 8, hand = 9.

MILLIONS
OBJECTIVE: To use approximation and estimation. To use written methods for long multiplication and division.
BEFORE: This activity links with work on place value and manipulating very large numbers. Stimulate the children's interest by asking them to make and justify guesses. Do a class survey of yes/no answers and reasonable guesses for each question. Make sure that at least one child will investigate each question.
AFTER: Go through the children's answers in the following week.

THE ANSWER TO EVERYTHING
OBJECTIVE: To use knowledge of multiplication facts (and place value) to solve a problem.
BEFORE: Along with 'Estimate', this activity should be left until the children are very confident with multiplication and place value. To make this homework task useful, provide a whole-class introduction that starts the children's minds going off in different directions. They need to understand that any number can be used (in combination with a decimal number).
AFTER: Create a class chart showing all the correct number sentences found.

FACTORS AND MULTIPLES
OBJECTIVE: To identify factors and multiples.
BEFORE: Play the game, using 1–100 cards spread randomly face up on the floor. Any number of children can play – perhaps in a circle around the cards, with you selecting a child to make each move. The first child to make the next player 'stuck' wins.
AFTER: The winning strategy has to do with prime numbers. Can the class find and explain it?

GRAB
OBJECTIVE: To identify multiples and know tests for divisibility. To use knowledge of number facts and place value to multiply and divide mentally.
BEFORE: Write up four digits and work through each property card with the class, rearranging the digits and talking through the reasoning. Then play with the class, using dice or 0–9 cards: make four digits, select a property card and then pick a child to write his or her answer on the board and justify it. Any child who makes the best possible number gets a point.
AFTER: Play the game again in class. Can anyone suggest any new property cards?

TEACHERS' NOTES

MULTISTEP & MIXED OPERATIONS

1999
OBJECTIVE: To use all four number operations to solve problems.
BEFORE: Do this as a whole-class mental maths activity, then introduce the homework. Show the class how using $\sqrt{9}$ opens up new possibilities. Can they suggest any other tricks?
AFTER: Create a class chart with all the children's answers.

1, 3, 5, 7, 9
OBJECTIVE: To use all four number operations to solve problems.
BEFORE: This activity follows on from '1999'. Present it as a genuine challenge: there is no definitive list of answers, and your class may well find new ones.
AFTER: Start a class chart and add to it as the homework returns.

FAIR SHARES
OBJECTIVE: To identify and use appropriate number operations to solve problems. To make reasonable estimates.
BEFORE: Model with the class how to approach the problem in a logical and systematic way (as shown in the 'Dear Helper' note). Ask the children for reasonable guesses; discuss how they reach them.
AFTER: Discuss the children's answers and strategies. The answer is: youngest £1050, next £1100, eldest £1150, mother £2300.

CALENDAR MAGIC
OBJECTIVE: To use all four number operations to solve problems.
BEFORE: This activity gives useful practice in following a sequence of instructions and reading charts. Go through the steps with the class, using that day's date and then a date that is important to the class.
AFTER: Find topic-related dates and ask the children to tell you what day of the week they came on.

MATHS TENNIS
OBJECTIVE: To practise instant recall of number facts for all four operations.
BEFORE: Introduce this game by writing a number (such as 56) on the board and inviting as many ways of making it as possible. Then add a grid of six numbers from which the children's answers must be drawn (using any operation). Play the game on an enlarged board or OHT. Emphasize that the number can be 'returned' in any way, not just by using factors.
AFTER: Discuss how the game went. Play it in pairs.

'STAY THE SAME' NUMBERS
OBJECTIVE: To reason and predict, using the relationships between number operations.
BEFORE: The children will need to have used function machines to find outputs, inputs and functions.
AFTER: Discuss the solutions found. The general solution is that the 'stay the same' number is the result of dividing the number in the second box by one fewer than the number in the first box.

MYSTERY SQUARE
OBJECTIVE: To identify and use number relationships. To approach a problem logically.
BEFORE: The sample problem can be solved by trial and improvement, using the information given about green. Model how to organize trial solutions based on an estimate of the 'green' number (as shown in the 'Dear Helper' note). Encourage the children to create their own mystery squares. Have a mystery square of your own prepared; read your clues to the class.
AFTER: Display the children's clues and unfolded squares. The answer to the sample problem is: green 20, red 40, white 38, blue 2.

SNAP!
OBJECTIVE: To recognize number relationships, generalize and make predictions.
BEFORE: The children will need to be used to investigating number patterns. Encourage them to work systematically – for example, to try (1, 1, 1), then (1, 1, 2) and so on. Alternatively, lead them into logical thinking that narrows down the field: *What is the biggest sum possible if you use numbers less than 10 for the answers to P = 2S? It is 27 (9, 9, 9) – but the product is far more than twice 27 (9 × 9 × 9 = 729).*
AFTER: Discuss the results. The solutions for P = 2S are (1, 3, 8), (1, 4, 5) and (2, 2, 4). Those for P = 3S are (1, 5, 9), (1, 6, 7), (2, 3, 5) and (1, 4, 15).

HAPPY BIRTHDAY!
OBJECTIVE: To use a range of mental calculation skills.
BEFORE: Try out this 'trick' on the class, choosing individuals who reveal their birthday to the class while you 'guess' the date. Then explain how to do it!
AFTER: More able children could find out how the trick works, using algebra.

6 STEPS TO 1000
OBJECTIVE: To choose and use appropriate number operations to solve a problem. To think strategically.
BEFORE: The children should have experience of playing calculator games. Let them practise playing the game in pairs. They may well realise that they can pick a start number which they have mentally calculated they can reach in six steps – if so, good!
AFTER: Discuss the children's scores and how they got them. You could then discuss ways of reaching 1000 exactly – for example, 12 − 3 − 1 × 6 + 2 × 4 × 5.

MENTAL MATHS HOMEWORK

SQUARE DANCE

YOU WILL NEED: A helper, a piece of paper, two pencils.

YOU ARE GOING TO: try to beat your helper by using your knowledge of square numbers.

❑ Write the digits 0–9 four times on a piece of paper, like this:

```
0 1 2 3 4 5 6 7 8 9
0 1 2 3 4 5 6 7 8 9
0 1 2 3 4 5 6 7 8 9
0 1 2 3 4 5 6 7 8 9
```

```
0 1 2 3 4 5 6 7 8 9
0 1 2 3 4 5 6 7 8 9
0 1 2 3 4 5 6 7 8 9
0 1 2 3 4 5 6 7 8 9
```

Jamie score	Lisa score	Running total
3		3
	4	5
5		5
	4	16
	5	25
		34

❑ Take turns with your helper to cross out a digit and say the running total of the numbers crossed out so far. If you reach a running total that is a **square number**, you score its **square root**. Keep a note of the running total and your separate scores.

For example: if you start by crossing out 9, you score 3 ($3 \times 3 = 9$). Your helper might then cross out 7 to reach a running total of 16, scoring 4 ($4 \times 4 = 16$). What might happen next?

❑ When no more moves are possible, add up all your square root scores. The player with the higher total score wins.

❑ Can you devise a strategy for winning this game? When might it be useful to cross out 0?

❑ Does the game get harder or easier to play as the numbers get higher? Why?

❑ Did you or your helper land on every possible square number?

❑ Find a winning strategy and be ready to explain it to your class at school.

YOU MIGHT LIKE TO TRY:

❑ Making the game easier by using only two rows of 0–9 (so $9 \times 9 = 81$ will be your top target).

❑ Making the game harder by adding more rows of 0–9 and aiming for even higher square numbers.

DEAR HELPER

THE POINT OF THIS ACTIVITY: is to recognize special patterns of numbers. This is an important aspect of becoming confident with numbers, and is a basic skill for algebra. Square numbers are special because they are formed by multiplying whole numbers by themselves (for example, $4 \times 4 = 16$).

Two symbols are important here. 4^2 means 4 squared (4×4). $\sqrt{16}$ means the **square root** of 16 (the number that times itself makes 16).

At this stage, your child should know all the square numbers to 12×12 by heart: 4, 9, 16, 25, 36, 49, 64, 81, 100, 121, 144.

Before starting this game, see how many square numbers you and your child can write out together from memory.

YOU MIGHT LIKE TO:
- Explore with your child how the $\sqrt{}$ (square root) button on a calculator works.
- Investigate which numbers under 100 are the sum of two square numbers. For example, $4^2 + 3^2 = 16 + 9 = 25$.

IF YOU GET STUCK:
- Use a reference list of square numbers.
- Discuss the different strategies you can use for this game. Is it always best to use up the 0s early on? Can you stop your opponent from scoring?
- Throughout the game, talk about the next square number that you are aiming for.

Please sign: . . . .

NAME

DATE

MILLIONAIRE

YOU WILL NEED: A helper, a calculator each. A referee might help!

YOU ARE GOING TO: use your knowledge of place value to be the first to score a million.

❑ Start by each entering a 6-digit number into your calculator. Each digit must be different (as in 512,768). Do **not** show your number to your helper at any time in the game!

❑ You start. Choose a digit from 1 to 9. Ask your helper: 'Give me all your...' and say your chosen digit. If you choose 6 and your helper's number is 342,673, he or she owes you 600. If the number is 654,879, you get 600,000! However, if the number is 234,589, your helper can say 'I don't have any.' (Now you see why you might need a referee!) You add the 'given' amount to the number on your calculator, while your helper subtracts it from his or her number.

❑ Now your helper chooses a digit and asks you for it.

❑ Carry on taking turns until one of you wins by reaching a score over a million (1,000,000)!

❑ As the game goes on, your number will keep changing. If the digit you are asked for occurs more than once in your number, you can choose which value to give your helper. So if he or she asks for 'all your 6s' and your number is 612,456, don't hand over 600,000 – just hand over 6! And if your number gets really low, don't let on!

❑ Be ready to talk about the game when you go back to school.

DEAR HELPER

THE POINT OF THIS ACTIVITY: is to help your child recognize very large numbers and appreciate that the value of a digit in a number depends on its position.

Before starting the game, practise putting large numbers into the calculator and saying them to each other. What is the biggest number your child can both enter and say out loud? Include tricky ones with zeros in, such as 1,008,070. Try the game together at first, looking at each other's numbers to get the idea of identifying values and doing the taking away and adding up. Play together in this way for as long as you like before having a competitive game.

YOU MIGHT LIKE TO: Think about a good start number. Why is starting with a number over 900,000 (such as 958,763) **not** a good plan?

IF YOU GET STUCK:
• Make the game easier by starting with a 3-digit number and aiming for 1000.
• Make a reference list like the one shown below. Put it where you can both see it. Use it to help you check the number of zeros you need to enter when you add or take away each number.

200,000
20,000
2,000
200
20
2

Please sign: . . . .

| NAME | DATE |

LENGTH CHART

YOU WILL NEED: A helper, a pencil, this page, some information about lengths and distances.

YOU ARE GOING TO: draw up a chart of comparative lengths.
❏ Look together at the chart below.

1,000,000 metres

100,000 metres

10,000 metres

1,000 metres (1km)

100 metres

10 metres

1 metre ⎨ Longest fingernail ever: 1.40 metres
         ⎩ Length of a normal school table for two

0.1 metre

0.01 metre (1cm)

0.001 metre (1mm)

❏ With your helper, try to think of something that is approximately each of these lengths or distances. Write them on the chart.
❏ Bring your completed chart into school.

YOU MIGHT LIKE TO TRY: adding some more measurements of your own, fitting them in the right places – the more unusual and unbelievable the better! *The Guinness Book of Records* is a great source for this kind of information.

DEAR HELPER

THE POINT OF THIS ACTIVITY: is to help your child estimate distances and lengths. This is an important practical skill. Having a few reference points – for example, knowing that the width of a little finger is approximately 1cm – can be useful in practical situations. This activity could be a lot of fun if you set about searching for unusual facts!

YOU MIGHT LIKE TO: Help your child use this activity to practise the rules of **place value**. Each step up from the bottom of this chart is 10× bigger, and each step down is 10× smaller (or ÷10). Ask: *How much bigger is 1 metre than 0.001 metres?*

IF YOU GET STUCK:
● Use a list of units for conversion. For metric distances, there are 10 millimetres (mm) in 1 centimetre (cm), 100cm in 1 metre (m) and 1000m in 1 kilometre (km). If you are used to working in non-metric units, 1 inch is 2.54cm, 1 yard is 0.9144m and 1 mile is 1.6093km.

Please sign: . . . .

COUNTING AND ORDERING

IMPACT

MENTAL MATHS HOMEWORK

PRIME TARGET 1

YOU WILL NEED: A helper, a pencil and paper.

YOU ARE GOING TO: investigate this statement:

Every number is either a prime number or the sum of two prime numbers.

❑ How could you test this statement? Start by looking at the numbers up to 50. Think about how you will organize yourself so that you can be logical and systematic.
❑ Bring your results, and any ideas you have developed about prime numbers, back to school.

YOU MIGHT LIKE TO TRY:
Memorizing as many prime numbers as you can.

1 - Impossible
2 - Prime
3 - Prime
4 - 2+2
5 - Prime
6 - 3+3
7 - Prime
8 - 5+3
9 - 7+2
10 -
12 -
13 -
14 -
15 -

DEAR HELPER

THE POINT OF THIS ACTIVITY: is to help your child learn the **prime numbers**. This is important, since they appear in school maths work at this level. Prime numbers are numbers which have only two **factors** (numbers into which they divide): themselves and 1. 2 is unique: it is the only **even** prime number (its only factors are 1 and 2). 1 is **not** a prime number, since it has only one factor.

This activity will also develop your child's sense of the need to be methodical and persistent when carrying out a mathematical investigation. The best approach to the task is to write a list of all the numbers from 1 to 50; then write 'prime' next to all the prime numbers; then note how you can make all the remaining numbers by adding two of the prime numbers.

YOU MIGHT LIKE TO:
● Set a time limit and investigate as many numbers as possible in that time.
● Learn all the prime numbers under 20 by heart.

IF YOU GET STUCK:
● Help your child to start with 1 and work up in a systematic way. A pattern will emerge, and the activity will become easier.
● It may help if your child puts two dashes next to each non-prime number to remind himself or herself to use two numbers.

Please sign: . . . .

PRIME TARGET 2

YOU WILL NEED: A helper, a pencil and paper.

YOU ARE GOING TO: find the best answer you can to this prime number problem.
❏ Can you solve the following problem?

Using each of the digits 1-9 once only, make a set of prime numbers that, when added together, give the lowest possible total. The total does not have to be prime.

❏ Write out a reference list of prime numbers to help you check that the numbers you choose are prime.
❏ Take your best answer back to school.

Oh no, 12 isn't a prime number.

```
  89
  67
  43
   5
 +12
 ---
 215
```

BET YOU CAN'T:
Find a set of prime numbers, as above, to make the **highest** possible total.

DEAR HELPER

THE POINT OF THIS ACTIVITY: is to help your child recognize and know by heart the prime numbers under 100, and be able to make reasonable guesses at what numbers over 100 might be prime by using his or her knowledge of times tables and multiples.

Prime numbers are numbers which have only two **factors** (numbers into which they divide): themselves and 1. This means that they do not appear in any times tables. Whereas 48 can be made by multiplying the right combinations of 1, 2, 3, 4, 6, 8, 12, 16, 24 and 48, 47 can only be made by multiplying 1 and 47.

This activity will reinforce and practise knowledge of prime numbers. Your child also needs to think carefully about how to attain the lowest possible total.

YOU MIGHT LIKE TO: Work out with your child all the prime numbers under 200.

IF YOU GET STUCK: Use the reference list of prime numbers (see activity) to support your child's work.

Please sign: . . . .

THE POINT IS 5

YOU WILL NEED: A helper; the 10 game cards and game board from page 15; two counters of different colours; a calculator (if you get stuck).

YOU ARE GOING TO: play a game that practises multiplying and dividing by 1, 10, 100, 1000 and 10,000.

❑ Choose a diamond on the top row of the game board. Place your counter on it. Your helper should do the same.
❑ Shuffle the 10 cards and place them face down. Pick up the top card.
❑ If you can make a number in a diamond that touches your current diamond with a side (not a point), you can move your counter to that diamond. So if you start on 50 and turn over ÷100, you could move down to 0.5.
❑ Now it is your helper's turn to pick up a card.
❑ The first player to reach the 5 at the bottom of the board wins.

RULES

❑ You may not move into a diamond if your helper's counter is already there.
❑ You may move your counter in any direction, but the diamonds must touch with straight sides.
❑ If you cannot use the card you turn over, you cannot move for that turn.
❑ Used cards are placed face up in a new pile. When all 10 have been turned over, reshuffle them and use them all again.

❑ Is there a best diamond to start from?
❑ Bring your ideas for a winning strategy back to school.

BET YOU CAN'T:

Ask your helper to point to a sequence of moves, while you respond with the right sum as fast as he or she can point.

DEAR HELPER

THE POINT OF THIS ACTIVITY: is to learn the important rule that ×10 moves a digit one place to the left, and ÷10 moves a digit one place to the right. This is the basic rule in our counting system. Each jump to the left multiplies the number by 10, so two places increases a number by 100 (10 ×10), and so on. Children quickly learn that one jump to the left is ×10 – but a very common error is to think that two jumps is ×20, three jumps is ×30 and so on.

YOU MIGHT LIKE TO: Ask your child some mental maths questions that involve multiplying or dividing amounts of money by 1, 10, 100, 1000 or 10,000.

IF YOU GET STUCK:
● It may help to draw out a chart for reference, as follows:

TTh	Th	H	T	U	.	Tenths	Hundredths
				0	.	0	5
				0	.	5	
				5			
			5	0			
		5	0	0			
	5	0	0	0			
5	0	0	0	0			

● Use a calculator to check the calculations.

Please sign: . . . .

THE POINT IS 5 GAMEBOARD

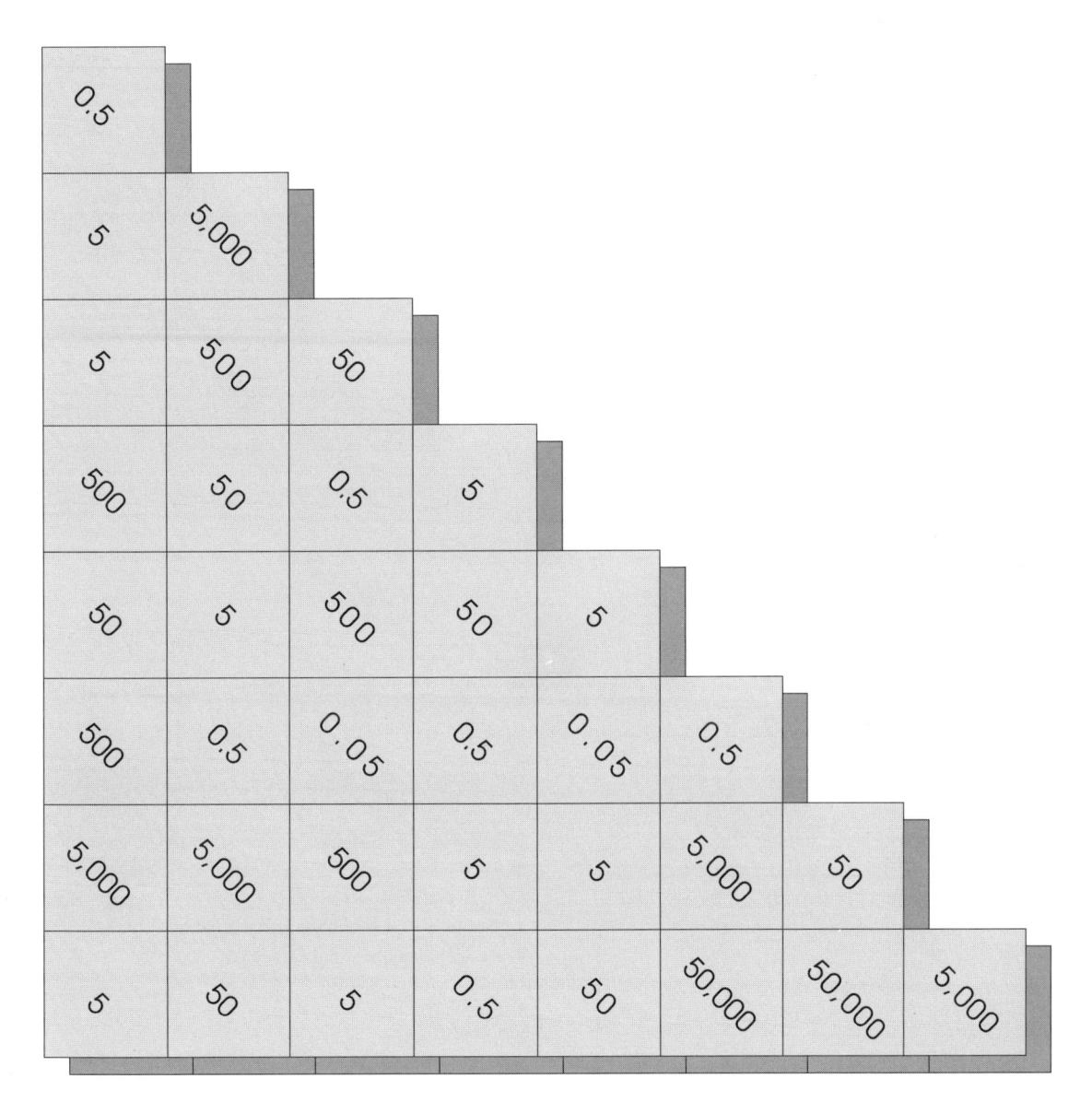

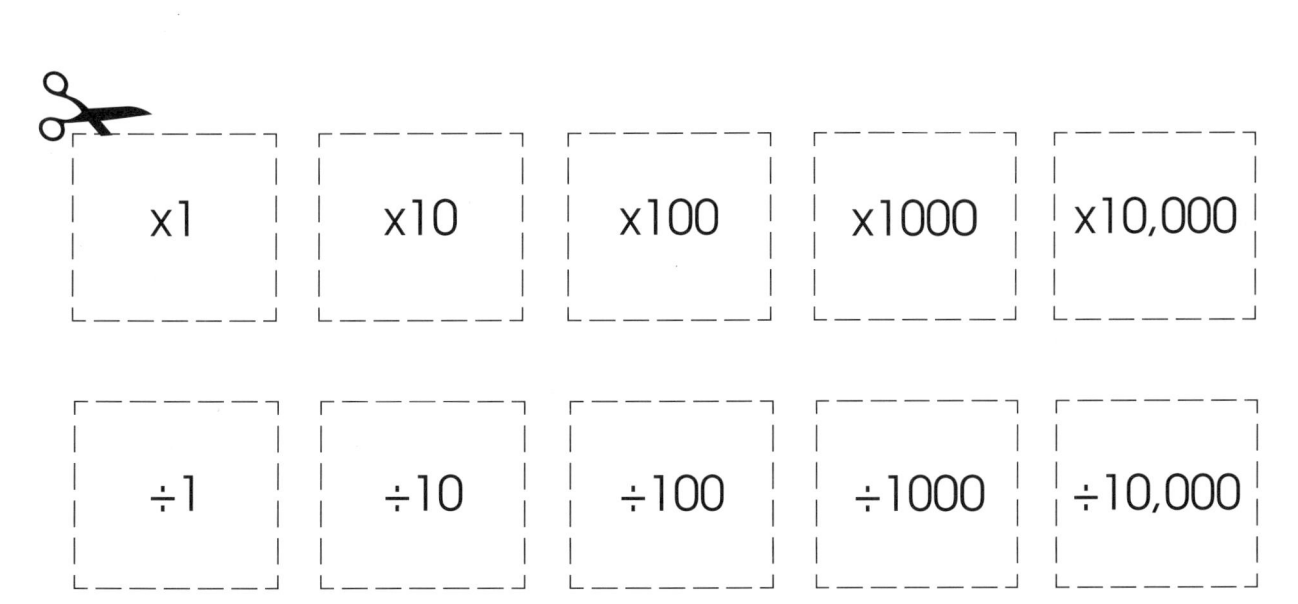

0.5							
5	5,000						
5	500	50					
500	50	0.5	5				
50	5	500	50	5			
500	0.5	0.05	0.5	0.05	0.5		
5,000	5,000	500	5	5	5,000	50	
5	50	5	0.5	50	50,000	50,000	5,000

✂

x1	x10	x100	x1000	x10,000

÷1	÷10	÷100	÷1000	÷10,000

NAME   DATE

DOES IT GO?

YOU WILL NEED: A helper, the game board on page 17, two dice, two counters, a calculator.

YOU ARE GOING TO: play a game that uses your knowledge of factors.
❏ Place both your counters on the start square. Take turns to roll the dice and add the numbers.
❏ If the number you roll is a **factor** of the next number on the board, you may move on a square. Otherwise, you stay where you are.
❏ Both players may have their counters on the same square at the same time.
❏ The first player to reach the end of the board (using the unshaded route) wins.
❏ If you roll a double, you have an extra turn.
❏ Next to each number on the game board, list the factors you or your helper rolled. Bring the game board back to school.

BET YOU CAN'T:
❏ Make the game much harder by using the shaded route. This includes very large multiples of 7 and 11. There are no easy tricks for dividing by 7 or 11 in your head! Here are two useful tests to see whether numbers with more than four digits are multiples of 7 or 11.

1. Find the difference between the last three digits and the rest of the number. If this number is divisible by 7 or 11, the original number is too. For example, look at 89,061:
89 – 61 = 28 which divides by 7, but not by 11
so 89,061 divides by 7, but not by 11.
Does this work for 13 as well?

2. Split the number into groups of three digits, starting from the right. Subtract and add these numbers in turn, starting with the left-hand number. Ignore any – sign in the result. If this number is divisible by 7, 11 or 13, the original number is too. For example, try 15,556,380:
15 – 556 + 380 = –161
161 ÷ 7 = 23
161 ÷ 11 = 14.636
161 ÷ 13 = 12.38
so 15,556,380 is divisible by 7, but not 11 or 13.

DEAR HELPER

THE POINT OF THIS ACTIVITY: is to practise how to spot whether a number is a multiple of each number from 2 to 12. By looking closely at, and learning by heart, the times tables to 10 × 10, it is possible to learn rules that allow you to recognize the multiples.
   A good way into this game might be to work out together, in advance, the factors from 2 to 12 of each number on the board. Use the rules listed below as a reference and write all its factors at the side of each number, so that you know what you need to roll.

YOU MIGHT LIKE TO: Write out **really** big numbers for each other and try out the tests of divisibility below.

IF YOU GET STUCK: Here are the tricks for seeing whether **any** number is a multiple of a number from 2 to 10. Test your child to see whether he or she knows them all! Multiples of:
• 2 – end in 0, 2, 4, 6 or 8.
• 3 – the digits always add up to 3, 6 or 9.
• 4 – if the last two digits (tens and units) are a multiple of 4, then the whole number is too.
• 5 – always end in 5 or 0.
• 6 – pass the test for multiples of 3 and are even.
• 7 – see above.
• 8 – if half the number passes the test for 4, the whole number is a multiple of 8. Or if the last three digits are divisible by 8, then the whole number is too.
• 9 – the digits always add up to 9.
• 10 – always end in 0.

Please sign: . . . .

DOES IT GO? GAMEBOARD

START
60
207
4,216
22
315
99
8,520
440
3,848
9,000
222
936
414
1,205
650
1,001,001
948
FINISH

ALTERNATIVE ROUTE
1,100
360
630
612
11,231
121
156
71,113
FINISH

COUNTING AND ORDERING

IMPACT

Mental Maths Homework

SUBTRACTAFACTA

YOU WILL NEED: A helper, a pencil and paper.

YOU ARE GOING TO: play a strategy game that uses your knowledge of factors.

❑ Agree on a start number. You identify a factor of that number and subtract it from the number to create a new number.

❑ Your helper now subtracts a factor of the new number. The game continues until someone reaches 0 and wins.

Note: you may not subtract the number itself unless it is 1.

Example game

Agree on a start number.		100
You subtract a factor of 100.	−10	90
Your helper subtracts a factor of 90.	−45	45
You subtract a factor of 45.	−5	40
Your helper subtracts a factor of 40.	−4	36
You subtract a factor of 36.	−18	18
Your helper subtracts a factor of 18.	−9	9
You subtract a factor of 9.	−3	3
Your helper subtracts a factor of 3.	−1	2
You subtract a factor of 2.	−1	1

Your helper subtracts a factor of 1 and wins, as that reaches 0 exactly!

❑ Bring your thoughts on a winning strategy back to school.

BET YOU CAN'T:
Work out a sure-fire way of winning!

DEAR HELPER

THE POINT OF THIS ACTIVITY: is to practise recalling times tables and factors. **Factors** are numbers that fit into larger numbers exactly, and **multiples** are larger numbers that can be made exactly with a number. So 2 is a **factor** of 10, and 10 is a **multiple** of 2. This game concentrates on factors. It also develops strategic thinking! As you play, talk about your moves: *I'm going to pick 4 as a factor of 40. 10 4s are 40. That leaves 36. You've got **lots** of choice there.* As your child selects a factor, ask how many of it fit into the number.

YOU MIGHT LIKE TO: Agree on a maximum start number. If you are both keen to work out a winning strategy, why not start with a smaller number?

IF YOU GET STUCK: Remember that you can always subtract 1, as 1 is a factor of any number. That might help you get to an easier number.

Please sign: . . . .

NAME   DATE

FRACTION CHANCE

YOU WILL NEED: A helper, two dice, a pencil and paper.

YOU ARE GOING TO: play a dice game involving fractions.

❏ Take turns to roll the two dice. Use the two numbers you roll to create a fraction less than 1 (for example, rolling 4 and 3 would give you ¾). If you get the same number on both dice, roll one dice again (you can choose which). Write down the fraction you create after each roll.

❏ If you can make exactly 1 by adding any of the fractions you have written down, then you win the game.

❏ Play until someone has won five times.

❏ Bring your score sheets back to school, where you will use them to investigate **equivalent fractions**.

BET YOU CAN'T

Change the rules so that the fractions you create are allowed to be **improper** (greater than 1). So a roll of 3 and 4 could be $\frac{3}{4}$ or $\frac{4}{3}$ (which is $1\frac{1}{3}$). This time, you win if you can make exactly 3 from your fractions.

DEAR HELPER

THE POINT OF THIS ACTIVITY: is to practise reading and writing fractions, particularly **equivalent fractions**. For example, $\frac{3}{6}$ is **equivalent to** (has the same value as) $\frac{1}{2}$. If you have $\frac{3}{6}$ written down and then roll a 1 and a 2, you win because $\frac{3}{6} + \frac{1}{2} = 1$.

Before you add fractions, remember to make sure that the **denominators** (bottom numbers) are the same. To do this, you multiply both parts of the fraction. For example, to add $\frac{1}{2}$ and $\frac{1}{6}$, you need to make $\frac{1}{2}$ into the equivalent number of sixths – so you multiply the 2 by 3 and then do the same to the top number (1). So $\frac{1}{2}$ is **equivalent to** $\frac{3}{6}$. The sum now reads: $\frac{3}{6} + \frac{1}{6} = \frac{4}{6}$.

YOU MIGHT LIKE TO: Use the Ace to 10 cards in two suits from a set of playing cards instead of the dice. Take turns to turn over two cards and create your fraction.

IF YOU GET STUCK: Draw up a list of equivalent fractions as a reference before you start:
$\frac{1}{2} = \frac{2}{4} = \frac{3}{6}$
$\frac{1}{3} = \frac{2}{6}$
$\frac{2}{3} = \frac{4}{6}$

Please sign: . . . .

NAME   DATE

DICEY DIVIDE

YOU WILL NEED: A helper, some counters, a Bingo board each (see page 21), two dice, a pencil and paper.

YOU ARE GOING TO: practise dividing small numbers by each other.
❏ Take turns to roll the two dice. Divide one number by the other to score a number on your Bingo board. Cover the number with one of your counters.
❏ The first player to place four counters in a row wins. You may not use a calculator, but you may use paper and pencil.
❏ Write down a list of all the ways that each number on the board can be made with the two dice. Take it into school.

BET YOU CAN'T:
Write out a table showing the **approximate decimal values** of all the fractions that you can make with the two dice – for example: $5/6 = 0.8\dot{3}$, $1/6 = 0.1\dot{6}$. (Note that $0.8\dot{3}$ means 0.833333.)

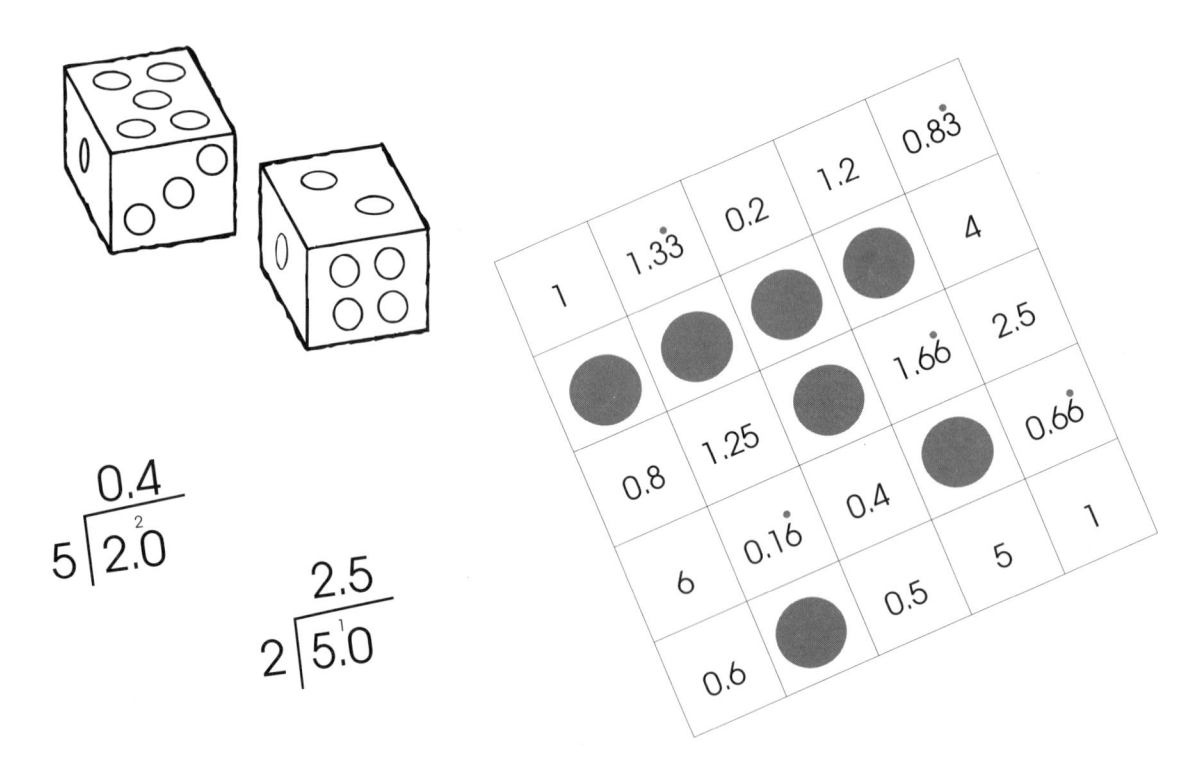

DEAR HELPER

THE POINT OF THIS ACTIVITY: is to practise division of small numbers to produce **decimal** numbers. It also encourages the development of **estimation** skills.

Children often get stuck at the stage of saying: 'You can't divide 3 by 5 – it won't go.' Encourage your child to make a reasonable guess at the two possible answers – for example, with 3 and 5: 'Well, 3 into 5 must be 1 and a bit, so I'll guess 1.66, and 5 into 3 must be a bit more than a half each, I'll guess it's 0.6.' If the answer is still not clear, work on paper using division (see the example illustrated above).

YOU MIGHT LIKE TO: Try to order all the numbers on the board from the biggest to the smallest.

IF YOU GET STUCK: Use a calculator.

Please sign: . . . .

DICEY DIVIDE: BINGO CARDS

1	1.3̇3	0.2	1.2	0.8̇3
1.5	0.75	1	0.3̇3	4
0.8	1.25	2	1.6̇6	2.5
6	0.1̇6	0.4	0.25	0.6̇6
0.6	3	0.5	5	1

1	1.3̇3	0.2	1.2	0.8̇3
1.5	0.75	1	0.3̇3	4
0.8	1.25	2	1.6̇6	2.5
6	0.1̇6	0.4	0.25	0.6̇6
0.6	3	0.5	5	1

BREAKFAST CHALLENGE

YOU WILL NEED: A helper, a box of cereal, a calculator, a pencil and paper.

YOU ARE GOING TO: work out the answer to this question:

How much of your favourite cereal would you have to eat to get 100% of your Recommended Daily Allowance of each of the vitamins it contains?

❏ Look on the side of the cereal box to find where it lists the information on **nutrition**. You should find a list of the essential vitamins that your cereal contains, such as Thiamin and Riboflavin. The packet will list what percentage of your RDA (Recommended Daily Allowance) an average bowl of this cereal with milk will provide.

For example, an average 30g bowl of a cereal might provide:
- 30% RDA of Thiamin
- 40% RDA of Riboflavin
- 25% RDA of Niacin
- 30% RDA of Vitamin B6
- 55% RDA of Folic Acid
- 75% RDA of Vitamin B12

So three 30g bowls of this cereal would give you 90% of your RDA of Thiamin, and another 10g would give you the final 10% – a total of 100g of cereal.

❏ Bring your answers, and the nutrition list for your cereal, into school. You will be comparing information on different cereals back in school.

YOU MIGHT LIKE TO TRY:
Comparing different cereals to see how much their vitamin content varies. Look at other food packets to see whether they give the same information. Find out what other foods provide these essential vitamins.

DEAR HELPER

THE POINT OF THIS ACTIVITY: is to consider the use of percentages in an everyday context. Looking at cereal boxes is a favourite breakfast pastime, and reading the nutrition lists is a valuable practical context for many areas of maths such as percentages and measures. Look at the nutrition list with your child and talk about it. Ask: *Which vitamins do you get more than half (50%) your RDA of in a bowl of cereal? Which do you get less than a quarter (25%) of your RDA of in a bowl?* Some amounts will be easier to calculate than others – for example, where it states that 30g gives 25% of the RDA, simply multiply 30g by 4. Encourage your child to find strategies for the more difficult calculations, instead of using the calculator.

YOU MIGHT LIKE TO: Look at other figures, such as the sugar, fibre or iron content.

IF YOU GET STUCK: Start by working out how much cereal provides 10% of the RDA. This is always useful, as it can then be multiplied by 10 (by means of repeated addition) to make 100%.

Please sign: . . . .

NAME   DATE

HAPPY NUMBERS

YOU WILL NEED: A helper, a pencil and paper.

YOU ARE GOING TO: use your knowledge of square numbers to find some **happy** numbers!
❑ Happy numbers zap to 1. Can you find some? This is how you zap!

Take any number – for example, 54. Square each digit and add them together: 25 (5 × 5) + 16 (4 × 4) = 41... Keep on repeating until you reach a single digit. If that single digit is 1, then the original number is happy!

Let's keep going with that example: 54 ➡ 25 + 16 = 41 ➡ 16 + 1 = 17 ➡ 1 + 49 = 50 ➡ 25 + 0 = 25 ➡ 4 + 25 = 29 ➡ 4 + 81 = 85 ➡ 64 + 25 = 89 ➡ 64 + 81 = 145 ➡ 1 + 16 + 25 = 42 ➡ 16 + 4 = 20 ➡ 4 + 0 = 4. So 54 is **not** a happy number.

However, 31 **is** a happy number, because 31 ➡ 9 + 1 = 10 ➡ 1 + 0 = 1. And what's more, it only took two stages!
❑ Who in your house is a happy age?
❑ Is your house or flat number happy?
❑ Are any prime numbers happy, or are they all miserable?
❑ Keep your eyes open for times when a number chain links into one you have already done. For example, you already know that 41, 50 and 29 are unhappy numbers. Trying them again won't cheer them up!
❑ Bring your results back to school.

BET YOU CAN'T:
❑ Sort your starting numbers by the number of stages it takes to reach a single digit. For example, starting from 54, it took 11 stages to reach a single digit.
❑ Make a list of all the happy numbers you find.

DEAR HELPER

THE POINT OF THIS ACTIVITY: is to help your child memorize square numbers. **Square numbers** are formed when a number is multiplied by itself (for example, 4 × 4 = 16). By the age of 11, children are expected to know the squares of numbers up to 12 × 12 (144) by heart. Activities such as these also help to develop a child's interest in number patterns, which is important for later work in algebra.

It would be a good idea to start this activity by writing out the squares of the numbers 1–9 together. If your child is doing well, you could hide them as the investigation proceeds!

YOU MIGHT LIKE TO: Use a long strip of paper to make a chain that shows how each number 'zaps' to the next.

IF YOU GET STUCK: Encourage your child to keep using the list of square numbers as a reference.

Please sign: . . . .

NAME   DATE

WHO DARES WINS

YOU WILL NEED: A helper, two dice, a pencil and paper.

YOU ARE GOING TO: play a dice game that uses addition.

❏ Choose who will start. If you are starting, roll both dice. Make a number, deciding which dice shows tens and which dice shows units (for example, a 6 and a 2 could be 62 or 26). Write down that number.

❏ Take turns to keep rolling new numbers and adding them to your number, creating your own running total.

❏ Every time your total reaches a multiple of 100 exactly, you score the number of 10s in that number. So you score 10 if you land on 100, 20 if you land on 200, and so on.

❏ When one player's total reaches or passes 1000 they score 100 for winning and the game stops. Add up any scores you collected on the way. The player with the higher score wins.

Here is a sample game in progress:

Score Caitlin	Alex Score	
21	41	
73	84	
138	100	10
174	144	
	155	

Ah! 6 and 2 – I can make 26 to get to 200 from 174!

HANDY HINT!

Look carefully at the two digits you roll. It may be that by making the smaller number, you can reach a running total which is a multiple of 100.

❏ Bring your best score into school!

BET YOU CAN'T:

Change the rule so that landing on a multiple of 50 scores the number of 10s in that number (so 50 scores 5, 100 scores 10, and so on).

DEAR HELPER

THE POINT OF THIS ACTIVITY: is to practise quick mental addition, and to use it to predict possible scores. Make sure that you and your child are well organized before you start. You will each need two columns on your sheet of paper: one for your running total and another for your points score.

YOU MIGHT LIKE TO: Change the rules by using only one dice, aiming for 100 and scoring on multiples of 10 (so 60 would score 6).

IF YOU GET STUCK: Take time before each roll of the dice to work out what number would take you to the next multiple of 100.

Please sign: . . . .

NAME _____ DATE _____

GOAL!

YOU WILL NEED: A helper, a pencil and paper.

YOU ARE GOING TO: work with your helper to try and solve this number problem!

❑ Here is some information about goals scored in the Kentish Town Primary School second team last year. Between them,

Anita and Bahrum scored 100;
Bahrum and Christopher scored 82;
Christopher and Dean scored 85;
Dean and Emma scored 90;
Emma and Christopher and Anita scored 110.

❑ If everyone scored a different number of goals, how many goals did each player score?
❑ Bring your answer back to school.

BET YOU CAN'T:
Make up a sports problem of your own to challenge your teacher!

DEAR HELPER

THE POINT OF THIS ACTIVITY: is to use mental addition skills and develop problem-solving skills. A good way into this problem is to establish **reasonable guesses**. Talk with your child and try to decide on a sensible first guess. For example, Anita scoring 69 and Bahrum 76 is not sensible, as they add up to over 100. Can you tell who scored more out of Christopher and Anita? How do you know?

Trial and error, refining guesses as you go, is the key to this problem. Work on it together and share your findings – for example, *A must be more than...* Alternatively, divide the work between you – for example, *You try A = 60, B = 40. I'll try A = 40 B = 60.* It will make the working out simpler if you call the children A, B, C, D and E.

YOU MIGHT LIKE TO: Make up a similar problem about goals, ages, weights or money in purses. Send it into school.

IF YOU GET STUCK:
• Make sure that you check your estimates on the last statement. If there were only the first four sums, there would be many correct answers! Once you have made guesses for A and B, each further answer follows from calculations. For example: *If A is 25 then B is 75. So if B is 75, C must be 7. If C is 7, D must be 78, and if D is 78 then E must be 12. So here goes: if I'm right, E + C + A will be 110. 25 + 7 + 12 = 44. Oh dear – start again!*
• If you have tried A = 60 and B = 40 and it didn't work, remember to try the same numbers the other way round: A = 40 and B = 60.

Please sign: . . . .

NAME   DATE
_____

PYRAMID PROBLEM 1

YOU WILL NEED: A helper, a pencil and paper.

YOU ARE GOING TO: try to complete the number pyramid below.
The digits 0–9 pair up to make five two-digit numbers in the five bricks at the bottom of this pyramid. Two of these numbers have been found for you.

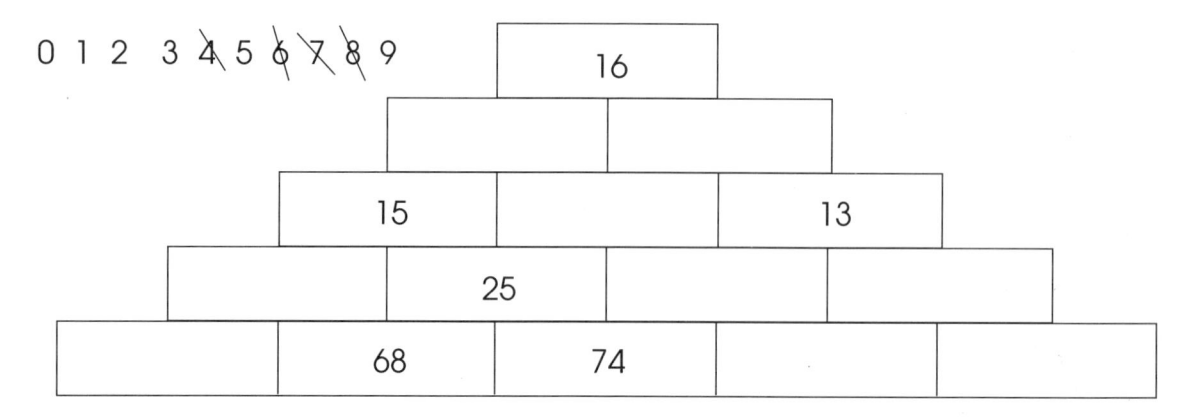

0 1 2 3 ~~4~~ 5 ~~6~~ ~~7~~ ~~8~~ 9

```
                    [    16    ]
                [        ][        ]
            [   15   ][        ][   13   ]
        [        ][   25   ][        ][        ]
    [        ][   68   ][   74   ][        ][        ]
```

❏ Can you complete the bottom row? Remember to use each digit once only.
❏ Now work your way up the pyramid, following this rule:

The number in each brick is the sum of the digits in the two bricks just below it. So the brick above 68 and 74 contains 6 + 8 + 7 + 4 = 25.

HANDY HINT!
Some of the bricks higher up the pyramid only hold single digits.

❏ Bring your solution (and your own problem, if you have made one) back to school.

BET YOU CAN'T:
Create your own pyramid problem by changing the base numbers. Once you have worked it out, draw another pyramid with only a few numbers revealed (including the top one). See whether your helper can solve this puzzle.

DEAR HELPER

THE POINT OF THIS ACTIVITY: is to develop your child's logical skill and perseverance with maths problems. Although the actual mental maths in this is relatively easy, your child has to do a lot of thinking!
   One way into this problem could be to start from the top: *What four digits add up to 16? Try 82 and 15 (8 + 2 + 1 + 5 = 16). But then again, are there four single digits that add up to 82? No. So maybe it's 28 + 15...*

YOU MIGHT LIKE TO: Have a race to see who can solve the problem first!

IF YOU GET STUCK:
● Draw some blank pyramids for your child. Young children lose interest if they get bogged down in drawing the pyramid.
● Encourage your child to write the digits 0–9 on a piece of paper and cross them out as he or she uses them. It is easy to use a digit twice in the bottom row by accident.

Please sign:. . . . .

NAME   DATE

PYRAMID PROBLEM 2

YOU WILL NEED: A helper, a pencil and paper.

YOU ARE GOING TO: work with your helper to create a number pyramid.

❑ Draw your own number pyramid, like the one shown below. Organize the digits 0, 1, 2, 3, 4, 5, 6, 7, 8 and 9 into five pairs on the bottom line. Work your way up the pyramid by finding the **difference** between each neighbouring pair of numbers and filling in the brick above them.
❑ Can you beat the top score of 12 in the example below?
❑ Bring your highest top score, with your working, back to school.

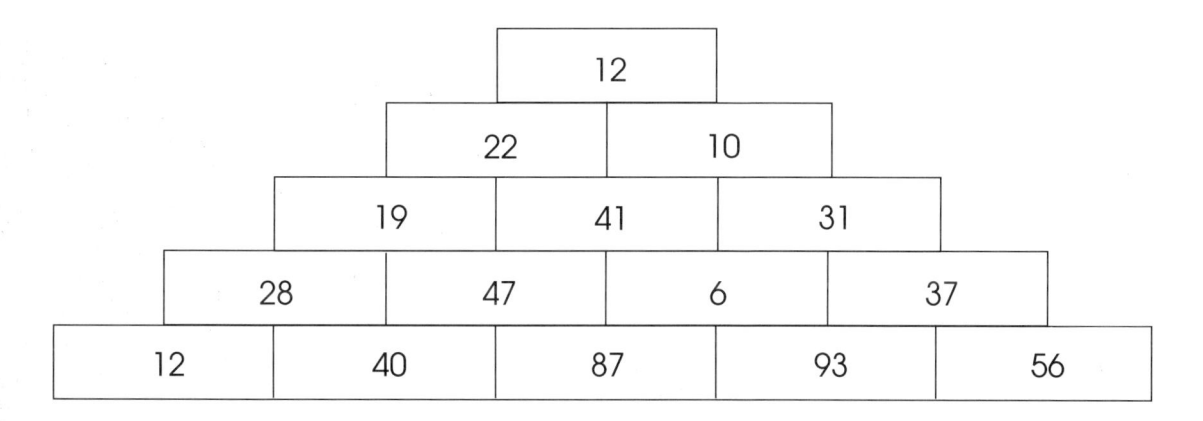

		12		
	22		10	
19		41		31
28	47		6	37
12	40	87	93	56

BET YOU CAN'T: Make a top score of 10, or even lower.

DEAR HELPER

THE POINT OF THIS ACTIVITY: is to increase your child's logical skills and perseverance. As the calculations involved are not too difficult, children can set about the task with confidence. Work on it together – or each make your own, but try to talk about the work. Talking is very important for developing confidence in maths.

YOU MIGHT LIKE TO: See how many different top brick answers you can make.

IF YOU GET STUCK:
● Help your child to draw the pyramids. Children can lose heart if they get bogged down with diagrams.
● To make sure that the top number is as high as possible, you need to make sure that the two numbers just below it are as far apart as possible. But remember that the bottom (starting) row must contain all the digits from 0–9.

Please sign: . . . .

TABLES PATIENCE

YOU WILL NEED: A helper; a pack of playing cards with the Kings, Queens, Jacks, 7s and 8s removed.

YOU ARE GOING TO: play a card game that practises multiplication.

❏ Shuffle the cards well, then lay out six cards face up in two rows of three. Hold the rest of the pack in your hand.

❏ Look for any pairs of cards (or groups of three or four cards) which you can multiply together to make either 36 or 60. Aces count as 1.

❏ When you see a combination, cover it with new cards from your hand. Explain to your helper why you are able to cover these cards. Put the new cards down face up. Now carry on looking for combinations.

❏ The aim of the game is to get rid of all your cards. If you get stuck and can't move, that game is over.

❏ Look at the example shown on the right. The player has got off to a good start, covering first 6 and 10 (6 × 10 = 60) and then 3 and 3 and 4 (3 × 3 × 4 = 36). What could be covered next?

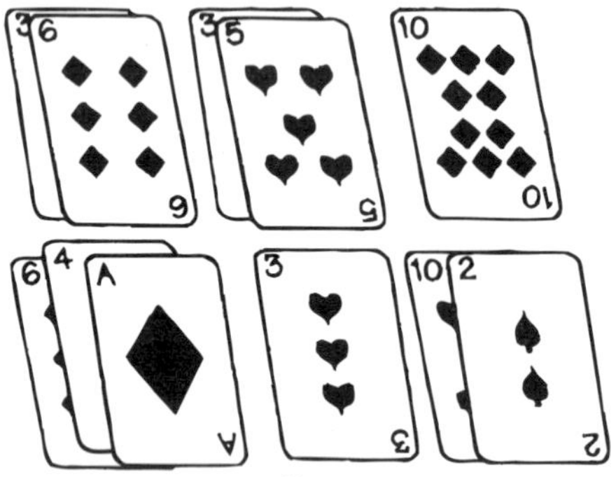

❏ Back at school, talk about how you got on.

BET YOU CAN'T:

❏ Change one of the target numbers to 12 or 24 or 100 or 48. (Add 7 and 8 back if they are factors of your new target number, and remove any cards that are not factors.)

❏ Explain why these are good numbers to use as targets.

❏ Explain why 31, 37 or 83 are bad numbers to use as targets.

❏ Make the game harder by using the same cards, but taken from two packs instead of one.

DEAR HELPER

THE POINT OF THIS ACTIVITY: is to practise multiplication skills. The cards used are all factors of 36 and/or 60. It is quite a challenge to get rid of all the cards, especially if you only look for pairs of numbers. Once you start to think in terms of three and four factors (as in 2 × 2 × 3 × 3 = 36), you have more chance of winning. This requires your child to multiply chains of numbers in his or her head, and to think strategically. The more reasoning your child does, the more likely he or she is to win. This requires your child to multiply chains of numbers in his or her head, and to think strategically.

YOU MIGHT LIKE TO:
• Make this a collaborative activity.
• Use two packs of cards and play against each other. The first player to run out of cards wins.

IF YOU GET STUCK: Help your child to write down all the possible ways of making 36 and 60 from the cards, and use this as a reference.

Please sign: . . . .

NAME _____   DATE _____

PYRAMID PATIENCE

YOU WILL NEED: A helper; a pack of playing cards with all the Queens, Kings and Jacks removed.

YOU ARE GOING TO: learn a new card game that helps you to practise times tables.

❑ Shuffle the cards well. Deal out five cards to form the bottom row of a pyramid. This row must have five different cards and no tens. Deal again if necessary.

❑ Hold the rest of the cards in your hand and turn over one card at a time. You may place each new card above and between two cards to form the next layer of the pyramid only if it is the **last digit** of the **product** of those two cards. Aces count as 1, and tens count as 0. For example:

❑ If you turn over a card that you can't use, discard it. The discarded cards may not be re-used.

❑ The aim of the game is to build up the rows until you can put one final card at the top of the pyramid. If you do this before you run out of cards, you have won.

❑ Back at school, report on how well you did.

YOU MIGHT LIKE TO TRY:
Allowing the pile of discarded cards to be reused once. This will make it easier to win!

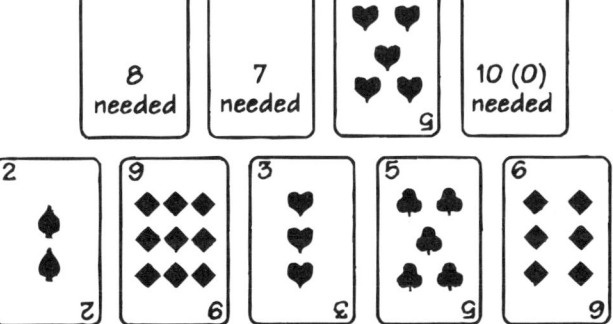

DEAR HELPER

THE POINT OF THIS ACTIVITY: is to practise instant recall of times table facts. This game is quite hard to win, and can become addictive! The best way to play is to think ahead at all times. Sit with your child and constantly ask *What do you need now?* Encourage your child to work out the answers to the pairs already in place, so that he or she knows what to look for in the next card: *So we need a 4 there (6 × 4 = 24), an ace there (7 × 3 = 21) and an 8 there (6 × 8 = 48).*

YOU MIGHT LIKE TO: Play an easier version of this game, in which you may add cards to the pyramid that are either the sum of **or** the difference between the two cards below it.

IF YOU GET STUCK: Use a written list of times tables as a reference.

Please sign: . . . .

NAME   DATE

THE WELSH BORDERS RACE

YOU WILL NEED: A helper, a pencil and paper.

YOU ARE GOING TO: use knowledge of times tables to solve a logic puzzle.
❑ Can you solve this puzzle with your helper?

The Welsh Borders Race is a major event in the horse-racing calendar. In this year's race, 36 heads and 108 legs left the start. At the third fence there were some fallers, and only 26 heads and 82 legs managed to carry on.
❑ How many horses carried on? How many still had riders?

2 miles later, the finishing line was crossed by 12 heads and 38 legs.
❑ How many horses finished the race without their riders?

❑ Bring your answers to the Welsh Borders Race puzzle back to school.

BET YOU CAN'T:
Make up a horse race problem of your own.

DEAR HELPER

THE POINT OF THIS ACTIVITY: is to use logic and knowledge of the multiples of 2 and 4. Each horse has 1 head and 4 legs; each rider has 1 head and 2 legs. So each horse and rider have 6 legs between them. Your child can use the starting figures to practise calculating: *36 heads left the start, so that must mean 18 riders (36 legs) and 18 horses (72 legs). So the total number of legs = 36 + 72 = 108.* He or she can use the starting figures to make answering the first question easier. To answer both questions, he or she must work out the answers through a process of trial and error!

YOU MIGHT LIKE TO: Try the traditional maths problem on which this activity is based. It goes as follows: *Looking out of the window, I saw some boys and dogs. Counting heads I saw 22, counting legs I saw 68. How many boys? How many dogs?*

IF YOU GET STUCK: Keep checking that your numbers of horses and riders always give the correct total numbers of heads and legs.

Please sign: . . . .

ESTIMATE

YOU WILL NEED: A helper, a dice, a pencil and paper.

YOU ARE GOING TO: practise your estimation skills.

❑ Roll the dice four times to give, in order of rolling, a thousands digit, a hundreds digit, a tens digit and a units digit. You now have a four-digit number. This is your target number.

❑ You and your helper now make one guess each at **two** two-digit numbers that multiply together to make the target number. You may **not** use calculators.

❑ When you have both had a guess, swap papers and work out the product of the numbers that your helper guessed. Whichever guess gives the closest product to the target number wins its player a point.

❑ You get a bonus point if your estimate is within 500 of the target number.

❑ The first player to reach 10 points wins.

BET YOU CAN'T:

Solve this example. Two players had the target number 5462. Player A guessed 59 × 91 and player B guessed 65 × 93. Who would get a point for this round?

(Illustration note: 2533 rounds to 2500 = 50×50 so guess 51×51)

DEAR HELPER

THE POINT OF THIS ACTIVITY: is to practise paper-and-pencil methods for long multiplication and to extend estimation (guessing) skills.

A useful strategy to help this game along is as follows. Round off the target number to the nearest thousands and hundreds number – so 5462 would round up to 5500. Look at the first two digits (55 in this case) and find two numbers which multiply together to give that number or a number close to it (in this example, 6 × 9 = 54). Multiply each of these numbers by 10 (in this example, 60 × 90 = 5400) to find a reasonable solution.

YOU MIGHT LIKE TO: Use a calculator to refine your original guesses until you reach the target number exactly – or as close as you can get with whole numbers. This is excellent practice for developing estimation skills and knowledge of number facts.

IF YOU GET STUCK: Use a calculator for checking estimates.

Please sign: . . . .

MISSION IMPOSSIBLE?

YOU WILL NEED: A helper, a pencil and paper.

YOU ARE GOING TO: solve a difficult number problem involving multiplication.

❑ You have been asked to go on a mathematical mission to Tipton Toy Superstore. You have been given £100 to spend. You have three choices of toys:
- Dribble Dolly – £26 each
- Yorky Yoyo – £1 each
- Slime Worm – 50p each

❑ You must spend **exactly £100** and buy **exactly 100 toys**, including at least **one** of each toy. What will you buy?

❑ Bring your answer back to school.

BET YOU CAN'T:
Make up your own shopping problem that involves buying 100 items and spending £100 exactly.

DEAR HELPER

THE POINT OF THIS ACTIVITY: is to practise multiplication skills. Your child will need to use mathematical reasoning to decide how sensible his or her guesses are. There are certain decisions you can make straight away to help the problem along – for example, the number of slime worms must be even (so that there is not an odd 50p left).

Once you have decided on these limits, finding the answer is a matter of trial and error. However, being organized about your trials will help greatly. Remember the double rule: 100 toys exactly **and** £100 exactly.

YOU MIGHT LIKE TO: Solve a similar problem that your child has invented.

IF YOU GET STUCK:
● Choose a combination of 100 toys that looks about right, then work out how much it will cost.
● Simplify the problem by focusing on the most expensive toys and working down to the cheapest.

Please sign: . . . .

NAME _____   DATE _____

GRIDLOCK!

YOU WILL NEED: A helper, a pencil and paper.

YOU ARE GOING TO: try and solve this devious number problem.
❑ In the grid below, each of the digits 1-9 is represented by a different symbol. The total of the numbers represented in each column or row is given at the end of it. Can you work out which digit each symbol represents?
❑ Bring your solution back to school.

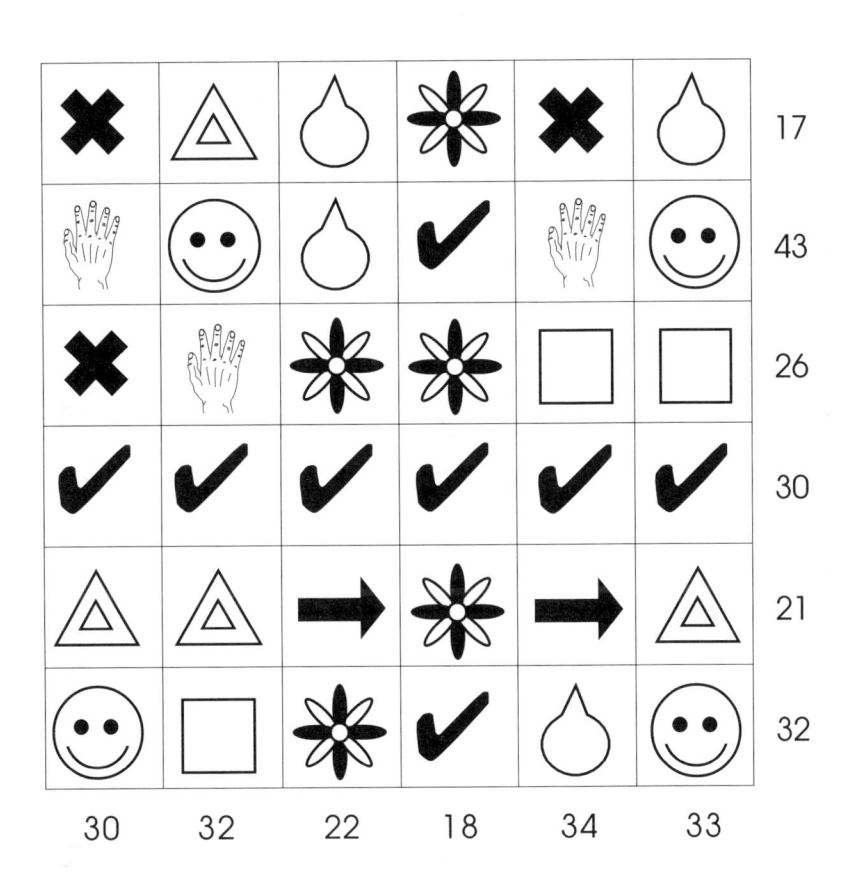

✖	△	◊	✻	✖	◊	17
🖐	☺	◊	✓	🖐	☺	43
✖	🖐	✻	✻	☐	☐	26
✓	✓	✓	✓	✓	✓	30
△	△	→	✻	→	△	21
☺	☐	✻	✓	◊	☺	32
30	32	22	18	34	33	

BET YOU CAN'T:
Make up a smaller 4 × 4 square problem of your own, using four symbols for digits.

DEAR HELPER

THE POINT OF THIS ACTIVITY: is to use logic and to test knowledge of times tables facts. The best way that you can help is to encourage as much talk as possible, in order to extend your child's thinking – for example: *If the triangle is 4, then 3 triangles = 12, so 2 arrows and a flower = 9. But is that possible?* or *Suppose the flower is 4, so 3 flowers = 12, so 3 ticks = 6. Does that work?* Encourage your child to work in a systematic way and to write down the digits 1–9, so that he or she can match up the symbols as each one is worked out.

YOU MIGHT LIKE TO: Help your child to devise a new multiplication grid with symbols representing the digits 1–9.

IF YOU GET STUCK: Look for the easiest place to start, a row where there is only one possible solution. Once you have this symbol matched to the right digit, you are off to a good start!

Please sign: . . . .

MENTAL Maths HOMEWORK

NAME _____	DATE _____

MILLIONS

YOU WILL NEED: a helper, a calculator, a pencil and paper.

YOU ARE GOING TO: answer a difficult question about the number 1,000,000 – that is, a million.

Who in your family has been alive for over a million hours?
Does a week's holiday last more than a million seconds?
How many pages does a million words take up in your reading book?
Could you run a million millimetres in an hour?
Have you slept for a million minutes during your life so far?

❑ Choose one of these questions. Take guesses from as many of your family as you can, then work it out! Did the answer surprise you?
❑ Bring your results back to school.

YOU MIGHT LIKE TO TRY:
Working out some more of these questions.

DEAR HELPER

THE POINT OF THIS ACTIVITY: is to practise the practical application of multiplication skills involving very high numbers. Stopping to reflect just how big a million is can be quite surprising! There are many opportunities in this activity for mathematical talk, as the most important parts of this activity are **estimating** the answer and deciding how to do the calculation.

YOU MIGHT LIKE TO: Start with the 'million words' question. Look at a real book. Agree on an **average** number of words per line and an average number of lines per page, then multiply these to find the average number of words per page. Divide 1,000,000 by this number to find the number of pages needed.

IF YOU GET STUCK:
• Let your child use a calculator. This activity is less about **doing** calculations and more about estimating and dealing with large numbers.
• The reference list below will be useful.

60 seconds in 1 minute   60 minutes in 1 hour
24 hours in 1 day   365 days in 1 year

100cm in 1 metre   1000 metres in 1km

1000 millilitres in 1 litre

Please sign: . . . .

THE ANSWER TO EVERYTHING

YOU WILL NEED: A helper, a pencil and paper, a calculator.

YOU ARE GOING TO: make up some number sentences.
When you were younger, your teacher may have asked you to think of as many ways as possible of making a number. Here's a harder version!
❏ Find at least ten ways of making **42**, using **multiplication only**. Write them around the 42 below.

42

❏ Bring your answers into school to help make a class chart.

BET YOU CAN'T:
Find ten ways of making **27**.

27

DEAR HELPER

THE POINT OF THIS ACTIVITY: is to extend your child's understanding of multiplication. There are various ways of doing this. One way is to start with 6 × 7 = 42 and then use knowledge of place value to find more answers, such as 0.6 × 70 = 42. Another way is to start with 6 × 7 = 42, then double 6 to get 12 and halve 7 to get 3.5. So 12 × 3.5 = 42. What happens if you double 12 and halve 3.5? A third way is to take any number less than 42 (for example, 20) and to work out, with the help of a calculator, how many of that number there are in 42. The answer will usually be a decimal number – for example, 20 × 2.1 = 42.

Encourage your child to use a calculator. It will not give correct answers unless the correct numbers are put in and the correct keys are pressed.

YOU MIGHT LIKE TO: Provide more target numbers.

IF YOU GET STUCK:
● Just do as much as your child is able to – you don't have to find ten ways.
● Start with a smaller target number, such as 10.

Please sign: . . . .

FACTORS AND MULTIPLES

YOU WILL NEED: A helper, a pencil each, the grid on this page, extra paper (if you want to play again).

YOU ARE GOING TO: play a strategy game using your times tables knowledge.
❏ Decide who is going first. That person, Player A, crosses out a number. The game **must** start with an **even** number.
❏ The other player, Player B, must now cross out and say aloud either a **factor** or a **multiple** of that number. It does not matter which.
❏ Now Player A must cross out either a factor or a multiple of the number that Player B crossed out.
❏ Carry on until one player is unable to move and loses. Once a number has been crossed out, it cannot be used again.

Here is an example of a game:
Player A 48
Player B 12 (4 × 12 = 48)   12 is a factor of 48.
Player A 3 (3 × 4 = 12)   3 is a factor of 12.
Player B 33 (11 × 3 = 33)   33 is a multiple of 3.
Player A 66 (2 × 33 = 66)   66 is a multiple of 33.
What number could Player B cross out next?

❏ If you want to play again, draw more 1–100 squares on blank paper.

❏ Bring your completed game, and your ideas about how to win, back to school.

1	2	3	4	5	6	7	8	9	10
11	12	13	14	15	16	17	18	19	20
21	22	23	24	25	26	27	28	29	30
31	32	33	34	35	36	37	38	39	40
41	42	43	44	45	46	47	48	49	50
51	52	53	54	55	56	57	58	59	60
61	62	63	64	65	66	67	68	69	70
71	72	73	74	75	76	77	78	79	80
81	82	83	84	85	86	87	88	89	90
91	92	93	94	95	96	97	98	99	100

BET YOU CAN'T:
Work out a definite strategy for winning every time!

DEAR HELPER

THE POINT OF THIS ACTIVITY: is to practise recalling the times tables and knowledge of factors and multiples.

Factors of a number fit exactly into it; **multiples** of a number can be made exactly with it. So 3 is a **factor** of 12, and 12 is a **multiple** of 3.

YOU MIGHT LIKE TO: Help your child find a winning strategy.

IF YOU GET STUCK: Use a written list of times tables.

Please sign: . . . .

NAME _____ DATE _____

GRAB

YOU WILL NEED: One or more helpers, a dice, pencils and paper, a set of 'properties' cards (cut out from this sheet), a small cloth or paper bag, a timer, a small toy that can be picked up easily and safely.

YOU ARE GOING TO: play a game to use what you know about numbers.

❑ Put the properties cards in the bag and shake them.
❑ Agree how much time you will allow for a round. Roll the dice four times to get four digits. Each player writes these on a piece of paper.
❑ Take a properties card from the bag and start the timer. Each player uses the four digits to create a number that fits that property. When a player thinks he or she has written the best answer, he or she grabs the toy and the round stops.
❑ If the player who grabs the toy has the best answer written down, he or she scores a point.
❑ Other players may challenge. If someone else has a better answer written down, he or she scores a point instead.
❑ If time runs out, that round is over and no-one scores. Sometimes, the round may be impossible – so no-one will score.
❑ The first player to reach 10 points wins.
❑ Take what you have written down back to school. Tell the class about your victories!

BET YOU CAN'T:
Play each round with a time limit of 10 seconds!

closest to 5000 when doubled	smallest possible even number	largest possible even number
smallest possible odd number	smallest possible multiple of 5	largest possible odd number
multiple of 3 **and** 4	smallest possible number	multiple of 4 and 5
closest to 5000	largest possible number	multiple of 3 **and** 2
largest possible multiple of 5	closest to 2000	

DEAR HELPER

THE POINT OF THIS ACTIVITY: is to use knowledge about numbers to solve problems quickly. Agree on a time limit that your child is happy with – 20 seconds is probably about right.

The numbers created will have four digits: thousands, hundreds, tens and units. A good way to start would be to roll the dice to get four digits, then work together to make the largest and the smallest possible number. You could also work through the properties cards, having a go together at finding a four-digit number to fit each property card.

YOU MIGHT LIKE TO: Try using these helpful tips.
● Multiples of 5 end in 5 or 0.
● If a number is a multiple of 3, the digits add up to 3, 6 or 9.
● To check whether a large number is a multiple of 4, look only at the tens and units (the last two digits). If this number is a multiple of 4, the whole number will be.
● Multiples of 2 are even, and so end in 0, 2, 4, 6 or 8.

IF YOU GET STUCK:
● Roll the dice three times. (You will need to adapt some of the properties cards to fit 3-digit numbers.)
● Play without a time limit.

Please sign: . . . .

1999

YOU WILL NEED: A helper, a pencil and paper.

YOU ARE GOING TO: investigate a number challenge.
❑ Use a pencil and paper to solve this problem:

How many numbers between 1 and 100 can you make as the answer to a number sentence using the four digits 1, 9, 9 and 9?

RULES
❑ Each number sentence must use all four digits once only.
❑ You may use the digits to form two-digit numbers, as in 99 − 19 = 80.
❑ No other digits may appear − for example, ^{2} as in 9^2 (9 squared) is not allowed.

❑ Bring your results back to school. In class, you will find out whether it is possible to make every number from 1 to 100!

HANDY HINT!
You can use any mathematical signs you like. For example, you could write:
$9 \times (\sqrt{9} \times \sqrt{9}) + 1 = 82$
or $1^9 \times (9 + 9 + 9) = 27$

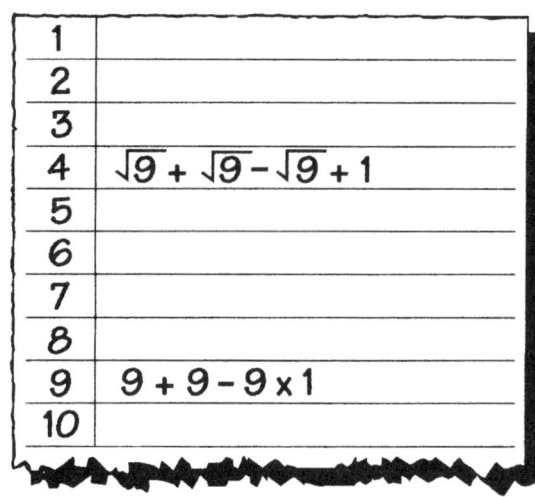

1	
2	
3	
4	$\sqrt{9} + \sqrt{9} - \sqrt{9} + 1$
5	
6	
7	
8	
9	$9 + 9 - 9 \times 1$
10	

YOU MIGHT LIKE TO TRY:
Asking at home whether anyone knows any other mathematical signs that might be useful.

DEAR HELPER

THE POINT OF THIS ACTIVITY: is that it can bring in a very wide range of number skills. It allows your child to use as much mathematical knowledge as he or she can in completing it. Help your child to organize his or her work. Draw a chart with the numbers 1–100 (or 1–50 if you prefer) written out. As solutions are discovered, they can be written by the appropriate numbers.

Encourage your child to try using brackets. These are very useful for constructing more complex number sentences. Brackets mean 'do this first'. For example,
$9 + 9 − 9 + 1 = 10$
but $9 + 9 − (9 + 1) = 9 + 9 − 10 = 8$.

Using the square root of 9 ($\sqrt{9}$) to make 3 is useful too.

YOU MIGHT LIKE TO: Help your child to make just 10 different answers, or to make as many numbers under 20 as he or she can.

IF YOU GET STUCK: Help your child to look for patterns – for example, try $9 + 9 + 9 + 1$, then $9 + 9 + 9 − 1$, then $9 + 9 − 9 − 1$, and so on.

Please sign: . . . .

NAME	DATE

1, 3, 5, 7, 9

YOU WILL NEED: A helper, a pencil and paper, a calculator.

YOU ARE GOING TO: make up some number sentences.
❏ How many different number sentences can you make that follow all of the rules below?

You must use the digits 1, 3, 5, 7, and 9. Every digit must be used once only. You may put digits together to make bigger numbers.
No other digits may appear – for example, ² as in 9^2 (9 squared) is not allowed.
The answer must be made up of the same digit repeated.
For example: $79 - 5 + 3 \times 1 = 77$.

❏ You may use a calculator for this – but remember that it won't always help.
❏ Bring your results back to school. See whether your class can come up with 20 different answers between them.

No, 68 isn't a repeated digit.

$57 - 1 + 9 + 3 = 68$

BET YOU CAN'T:
Make ten different answers. (If you can – well done!)

DEAR HELPER

THE POINT OF THIS ACTIVITY: is to challenge your child to use all his or her mental maths skills. It is possible to make several answers under 100, so encourage your child to stick with smaller numbers rather than very large numbers.

YOU MIGHT LIKE TO: Try making repeating-digit numbers over 100. What is the highest repeating-digit number you can make using 1, 3, 5, 7 and 9?

IF YOU GET STUCK: Keep a note of your child's attempts. If you suddenly hear a cry of *I've done it!* but when you say *Great – how?* the answer is *I can't remember*, it will be frustrating!

Please sign: . . . .

FAIR SHARES

YOU WILL NEED: A helper, a pencil and paper.

YOU ARE GOING TO: use your mental maths skills to solve a hard problem involving money.

❏ Can you solve this puzzle?

Mrs Share and her three children agree that if she ever wins with her premium bonds, they will share the winnings in the following way:
1. Round the winnings off to the nearest £100.
2. Each of the three children will get £50 more than the next youngest child.
3. Their mother will get twice as much as the oldest child.

To their great delight, they win £5,624. How much does each member of the family receive?

❏ Bring your answer back to school.

DEAR HELPER

THE POINT OF THIS ACTIVITY: is to use skills of estimation and basic number skills as well as developing techniques and attitudes towards problem solving and applied maths.

It is most satisfying to solve this problem! It can be done with algebra (writing equations in which the youngest child gets *x* pounds) – but it will be just as effective to use a process of trial and improvement, refining guesses each time (as in the example below).

YOU MIGHT LIKE TO: Set your child the challenge of solving it within 5 goes. This will really refine his or her guesses!

IF YOU GET STUCK: Help your child to be organized! What is £5,624 rounded off to the nearest hundred? Let's call the children A, B and C and the mother M. What must the units digit be in each amount? Why? Start by estimating what the youngest child (A) might receive. Write your estimates like this:
If A gets 400
B gets 450 (£50 more)
C gets 500 (£50 more)
M gets 1000 (double the eldest child)
Total: £2,350.
Too low – try a higher start number for child A.

It will help your child if you talk through the different stages each time:
Let's try £500 for Child A. So what will B get? Good. And C? Good. And double for Mother is...? Now let's add it up. Oh, too low again. What shall we try next?

Please sign: . . . .

NAME   DATE
_____

CALENDAR MAGIC

YOU WILL NEED: A helper, a pencil and paper.

YOU ARE GOING TO: learn some mathematical magic!

❏ What day of the week were you born? What day of the week will your 18th birthday be on? Did the First World War start on a Monday?

Here is a mathematical way of finding out exactly which day of the week any date in history (since 1725) fell on – and which day any future date will fall on!

❏ You will need to refer to these three charts:

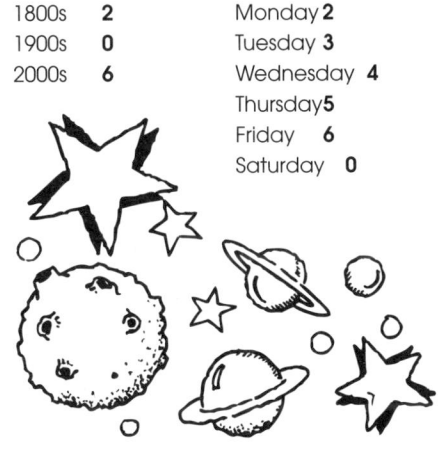

Chart 1		Chart 2		Chart 3	
1725 – 1799	4	Sunday	1	January	1 (0)
1800s	2	Monday	2	February	4 (3)
1900s	0	Tuesday	3	March	4
2000s	6	Wednesday	4	April	0
		Thursday	5	May	2
		Friday	6	June	5
		Saturday	0	July	0
				August	3
				September	6
				October	1
				November	4
				December	6

❏ Choose the date you want to investigate (for example, 25th December 2005).
(a) Write the last two digits of the year. (05)
(b) Divide the answer to (a) by 4. Ignore any remainder. (1)
(c) Look for the month code in Chart 3. If your year is a leap year (it divides equally by 4), use the bracketed code numbers for January and February. Write it down. (6)
(d) Write down the date of the month. (25)
(e) Add the century code from Chart 1. (6)
(f) You should now have a list of five numbers. Add them all up. (5 + 1 + 6 + 25 + 6 = 43)
(g) Divide your result from (f) by 7 and put the remainder in a circle. (7 into 43 goes 6 remainder 1).
(h) Now refer to Chart 2 to find which day of the week the remainder is the code number for! We have discovered that Christmas Day 2005 will be on a Sunday.

❏ Now answer the four questions below. Bring your answers back to school.

What day of the week was Christmas Day 1900?
Was the solar eclipse on a Tuesday (on August 11th 1999)?
On what day of the week did the Second World War start (3rd September 1939)?
Was it a Monday when Neil Armstrong – the first person to do this – stepped onto the moon (20th July 1969)?

YOU MIGHT LIKE TO TRY:
Finding out what days of the week your friends and family were born on.

DEAR HELPER

THE POINT OF THIS ACTIVITY: is to practise a range of mental maths skills through an intriguing puzzle. Have lots of practice goes together, so that you both try the hard bits!

Work through some examples together on paper to give your child practice with the calculations. Then let him or her have a go at working alone on the four questions.

YOU MIGHT LIKE TO: Think of lots of other dates for your child to find, including some where you already know the day of the week.

IF YOU GET STUCK: Write out each step carefully and talk through the stages slowly.

Please sign: . . . .

MULTISTEP AND MIXED OPERATIONS

IMPACT

41

MENTAL MATHS HOMEWORK

NAME   DATE

MATHS TENNIS

YOU WILL NEED: A helper, the gameboard on this sheet, two pencils, some paper.

YOU ARE GOING TO: do some keep-fit calculations!

❑ Play a game of maths tennis with your helper. Player A 'serves' by circling any number on the board. Player B must 'return' by crossing out, as quickly as possible, any combination of numbers that make that number in any way. Take turns to serve.

RULES

❑ You can use any mathematical operation:
+, −, ×, ÷.

❑ Any amount of numbers can be crossed out in a 'return'.

❑ Set a time limit – 15 seconds is about right, but make it longer at first if you want to. If you can 'return' in time you score a point. If not, your opponent does.

❑ If your return doesn't make the target number, your opponent scores a bonus point.

❑ The player who has more points when the gameboard is used up wins.

45	3	5	10	15	27	13	4	2	8
3	16	6	26	21	9	6	7	33	5
27	2	4	28	3	5	3	6	23	8
15	2	7	8	99	22	2	60	8	14
5	3	5	21	5	6	18	12	36	7
5	70	7	4	33	7	6	27	2	5
11	4	9	1	6	3	21	33	3	27
8	5	6	7	27	9	3	5	15	10
33	5	5	26	2	10	33	4	3	2
9	26	6	19	5	32	7	10	16	6

❑ Keep a record of how you made the numbers on paper.

❑ Bring your ways of making the numbers back to school, ready for a class match!

BET YOU CAN'T:
Choose a number on the board and find out how many different ways you can make it.

DEAR HELPER

THE POINT OF THIS ACTIVITY: is to practise mental calculation strategies at speed. Agree on a 'return' time that is appropriate for your child.

Have a non-competitive game to start with: name a number on the board, but don't cross it out. Can your child 'return'?

YOU MIGHT LIKE TO: Encourage your child to investigate how many different returns are possible for a given number. So, if you served with 33, a possible return might be 3 × 10 + 3 or 3 × 11 or 6 × 6 − 3 or 4 × 7 + 5. Talk about all the answers you can find to give your child as many ideas as possible.

IF YOU GET STUCK:
● Support your child by 'aiming' your serves at his or her ability level.
● Play initially without a time limit, to reduce stress!

Please sign: . . . .

NAME   DATE

'STAY THE SAME' NUMBERS

YOU WILL NEED: A helper, a pencil and paper.

YOU ARE GOING TO: investigate some number patterns.

If you put 4 into this function machine, it stays the same:

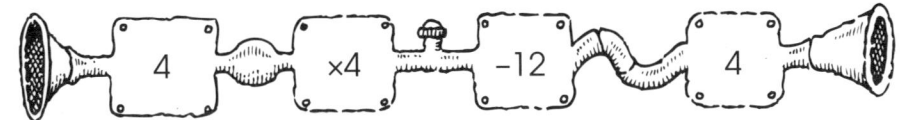

[4] → [×4] → [−12] → [4]

❏ Can you find a number that stays the same in this function machine?

[ ] → [×5] → [−20] → [ ]

❏ Or this one?

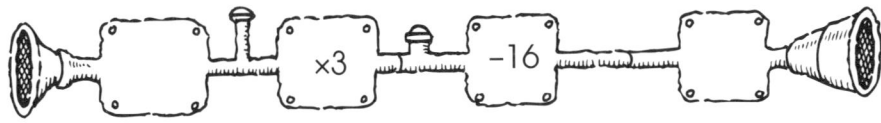

[ ] → [×3] → [−16] → [ ]

❏ Or this one?

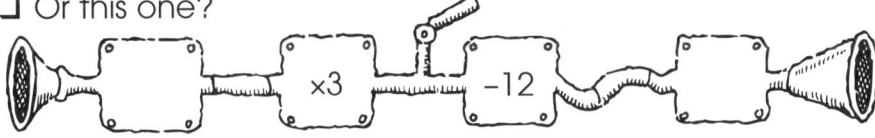

[ ] → [×3] → [−12] → [ ]

❏ Or this one?

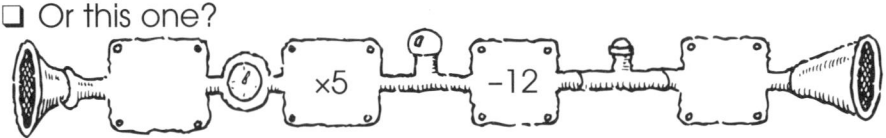

[ ] → [×5] → [−12] → [ ]

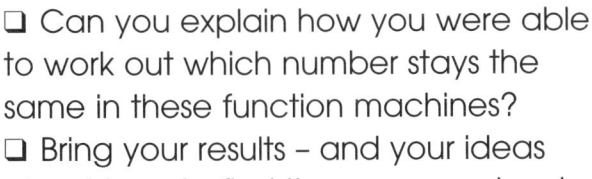

❏ Can you explain how you were able to work out which number stays the same in these function machines?

❏ Bring your results – and your ideas about how to find the answers – back to school.

BET YOU CAN'T:
Solve this one:

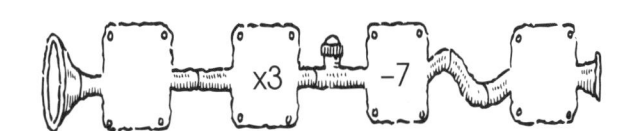

[ ] → [×3] → [−7] → [ ]

DEAR HELPER

THE POINT OF THIS ACTIVITY: is to think about the mathematical rules which are used to make patterns and sequences. This is an important skill in **algebra**. Only one number can be put into each of these **function machines** and come out the same. There is a consistent relationship between the one unchanged number and the two numbers in the machine.

YOU MIGHT LIKE TO: Give your child different output numbers for the function machines and see whether he or she can work out what numbers you have put in.

IF YOU GET STUCK:
● Simply give your child a number to input on each machine, and ask him or her to calculate the output mentally.
● Do not insist on a fully expressed answer to the final question. If your child can begin to predict what number 'stays the same', help him or her to put this thinking into words, then write it down and send it back to school.

Please sign: . . . .

MULTISTEP AND MIXED OPERATIONS

IMPACT

MENTAL MATHS HOMEWORK

MYSTERY SQUARE

YOU WILL NEED: A helper; red, green and blue coloured pencils or pens; the blank 100 square below.

YOU ARE GOING TO: make up a number puzzle to take back to school.
❑ On the grid below, colour some squares green, some red and some blue. Leave some white. For example, you might colour 30 green, 45 red and 15 blue, leaving 10 white.
❑ Now think about how many squares are in each colour. How could these four numbers be related to each other? Think of a way to state your colouring as a puzzle, choosing a basic colour to which all the others are connected. For example, using green as the basic colour:

'On my square, there are 100 squares – red, white, blue and green. There are twice as many red squares coloured as green squares, 18 more white squares than green squares, and 10 times more green squares than blue squares. How many squares are there in each colour?'

❑ Cut out the square, fold it into quarters and seal it! Write your clues on the outside. Challenge your helper to solve the puzzle. This will help you to check that your clues work!

❑ Bring your mystery square back to school – sealed, with your clues on the outside.

BET YOU CAN'T:
Write two different sets of clues for the same colour combination.

DEAR HELPER

THE POINT OF THIS ACTIVITY: is to encourage your child to solve problems through trial and improvement. This will help to develop your child's confidence and perseverance with maths problems.

YOU MIGHT LIKE TO: Try solving the example above with simple algebra, but only if your child is very confident.

IF YOU GET STUCK:
● Make sure that your child writes his or her clues using one colour as a basis, and uses all 100 squares in his or her puzzle.
● Let your child try out his or her puzzle on you first before writing it out neatly to take back to school.

Please sign: . . . .

SNAP!

YOU WILL NEED: A helper, a pencil and paper.

YOU ARE GOING TO: investigate some unusual sets of numbers.

1, 2, 3 is a special sequence, because 1 + 2 + 3 = 1 × 2 × 3. This is the only set of three numbers where this works.

However, there are **three** sets of three numbers where, if you multiply them together, the answer is **twice** as big as if you add them together: P (the product) = 2S (twice the sum).

For example, try 2, 5, 6.
2 + 5 + 6 = 13 and 2 × 5 × 6 = 60, so this doesn't work: 2 × 13 is not 60 (the product is not twice the sum).

❏ Can you find any of these sets of numbers?
❏ Bring your results back to school.

HANDY HINT!
In each of the three possible answers, the three numbers are all less than 10.

BET YOU CAN'T:
Find all three possible sets of numbers!

DEAR HELPER

THE POINT OF THIS ACTIVITY: is to get used to letters representing unknown numbers. This is an important step in algebra. Solving this maths problem requires logic and perseverance. One useful strategy is **trial and improvement**. Help your child to be **methodical** and encourage him or her to learn from each unsuccessful try. For example, he or she might try (1, 4, 7) and say: Right, the sum is 12 (1 + 4 + 7) and the product is 28 (1 × 4 × 7). Is 28 twice 12? No, but it's just over, so I'll try (1, 4, 6).

YOU MIGHT LIKE TO: Try finding the **four** sets of numbers where the product is **three** times as big as the sum (P = 3S). Again, all the numbers (except one) are less than 10.

IF YOU GET STUCK: Try this simpler problem. *How many sets of 3 numbers can you find that total 20?*

Please sign: . . . .

HAPPY BIRTHDAY!

YOU WILL NEED: A helper, a pencil and paper.

YOU ARE GOING TO: learn a mathematical mind-reading trick!
❑ This is a way of finding out the date of a person's birthday using your own (and someone else's) brilliant mental maths. Give your helper a pencil and paper, then ask him or her to follow these steps:

1. Write down the date of someone's birthday (that your helper knows and you don't) as two numbers: the month number (January is 1, February is 2, and so on), and the day number (for example, the 5th would be 5).
2. Multiply your month number by 5.
3. Add 7.
4. Multiply by 4.
5. Add 13.
6. Multiply by 5.
7. Add the day of the month. Write down the answer.

❑ When your helper gives you his or her answer, you mentally subtract **205** from it. The tens and units digits give you the day, and the hundreds (or thousands and hundreds) digits give you the month!
❑ Try doing these steps to prove to yourself that it works before you try it out. For example, for the 4th September:

1. Month number is 9, day number is 4.
2. 9 × 5 = 45
3. 45 + 7 = 52
4. 52 × 4 = 208
5. 208 + 13 = 221
6. 221 × 5 = 1105
7. 1105 + 4 = 1109
Then 1109 − 205 = 904. The tens and units (04) give the day: **the 4th**.

The other digit (9) gives the month: **September**. It works!
❑ Bring your stories of who you amazed back to school!

BET YOU CAN'T:
Use this mind-reading trick to find out the birthdays of some of the school staff!

DEAR HELPER

THE POINT OF THIS ACTIVITY: is to practise a range of mental maths skills, and to boost your child's confidence by letting him or her perform an impressive trick with numbers. Practise together several times, so that you both do the hard bits!

Once your child is confident with the mental subtraction of 205, let him or her try out the trick on friends and neighbours.

YOU MIGHT LIKE TO: Challenge your child to choose some dates for you to discover. That way, he or she will have to do the hard calculations unaided.

IF YOU GET STUCK: Work through some examples together on paper to practise the calculations.

Please sign: . . . .

SIX STEPS TO 1000

YOU WILL NEED: A helper, a pencil and paper, a calculator.

YOU ARE GOING TO: play a calculator game.

❏ Tap a two-digit number of your choice into the calculator. Then write the digits 1 2 3 4 5 6 on a piece of paper.

❏ Your helper now picks any number operation and a digit from the 1–6 list, and enters both of these on the calculator.

❏ You now do the same with another number operation and another digit from the list.

❏ Carry on doing this until all six digits have been used up. You are **working together**, and the aim is to end up with an answer as close to **1000** as possible. You must use all six digits, once only.

Here is an example:
1 2 3 4 5 6
42 is the start number.

42 × 6 = 252
252 × 4 = 1008
1008 − 5 = 1003
1003 − 3 = 1000
1000 − 2 = 998
998 + 1 = 999

❏ Play this as a game. Take turns to select a start number. Your joint score for each try is the difference between 1000 and the number you end up with. Play five rounds. A total score less than 5 is **GENIUS** level!

❏ Bring your best score back to school. Try to remember and write down how you got it.

BET YOU CAN'T:
Work out six steps to guarantee a score of zero!

DEAR HELPER

THE POINT OF THIS ACTIVITY: is to practise a range of mental maths skills and strategic thinking. Work together and talk about your plans. Is it always a winning strategy to start by multiplying until you get as close as possible to 1000? It's important to think ahead: remember, you must use all six digits. Plan what you will do mentally or by jotting ideas down on paper. Once you have entered your move into the calculator, you cannot change your mind.

YOU MIGHT LIKE TO: Help your child with the challenge of working out six steps that will guarantee a score of zero.

IF YOU GET STUCK: Avoid using division, which is liable to create fractional numbers. It is hard to get back from fractions to whole numbers.

Please sign: . . . .

Dear Parent

We all know that parents are a crucial factor in their children's learning. You can make a huge difference to your child's education. We are planning to send home some activities that fit in with the maths we are doing in school. The activities are designed for your child to do with you, or another available adult. You do not need to know a lot of maths in order to help your child.

These are not traditional homework activities. It is important that your child first explains the activity to you. Each activity will have been explained thoroughly in school. Then do the activity together. By sharing these activities with your child, you will be helping to develop her or his mental maths. And as a result of being given that all-important attention, your child is more likely to become confident and skilled in maths.

We hope, too, that these activities will be fun to do – it matters that children develop positive attitudes to maths. If you are particularly nervous about maths, try not to make your child nervous too! If your child is having difficulties, look at the 'If you get stuck' suggestions which are provided on each activity sheet.

After completing each activity, your child will usually have something to bring back to school. However, sometimes there may not be anything written down to bring back – your child is doing mental maths, so all the work may be in your heads!

If you have any problems with or further questions about any of the activities – or about any of the maths being covered – please do let us know at school. We do very much value your support.

Yours sincerely